Evaluating Campaign Quality

For a number of years, voters and academic observers have been dissatisfied with a number of elements of American campaigns. Contemporary races are seen as too negative, too superficial, and too unfair or misleading. Based on these complaints, a variety of reform organizations have targeted millions of dollars to improve the situation. Through their efforts and those within the academic community, a wide range of reform initiatives have been undertaken, such as voluntary codes of conduct, industry self-regulation, certificate programs, tougher ethics rules for consultants, and the encouragement of more substantive venues. Candidate debates, town meetings, and issue forums have been promulgated to improve the performance of American elections.

This book seeks to evaluate whether these activities have improved the level of campaign discourse and conduct in U.S. House and Senate campaigns and argues that while individual reform efforts have achieved some of their stated objectives, the overall effect of these reform efforts has been disappointing. A different approach to campaign conduct and political discourse in American elections is clearly called for if improved campaigning is the goal.

A former candidate for congress and a Democratic Party activist, L. Sandy Maisel is the author of *From Obscurity to Oblivion: Running in the Congressional Primary*; *Parties and Elections in America: The Electoral Process*; and *Two Parties – or More? The American Party System* (with John Bibby). Among the books he has edited and contributed to are *The Parties Respond: Changes in American Parties and Campaigns*; *Jews in American Politics*; and *Political Parties and Elections in the United States: An Encyclopedia*. Maisel also serves as editor for the new *On Politics* series. He and his wife, Patrice Franko, are currently at work on a book entitled *Fore and After: Signature Holes and Signature Dishes from the World's Great Golf Resorts*.

Darrell M. West is the author of 14 books dealing with media, elections, and technology policy. Among these are *Air Wars: Television Advertising in Political Campaigns*; *Patrick Kennedy: The Rise to Power*; *The Rise and Fall of the Media Establishment*; *Celebrity Politics*; and *Digital Government: Technology and Public Sector Performance*. He has given talks in a number of countries around the world and is a frequent commentator on media and elections.

Brett M. Clifton is Assistant Director of Administration and Programs and Lecturer in Public Policy at the Taubman Center for Public Policy at Brown University. His scholarly articles have appeared in *Political Science Quarterly* and *Party Politics*. His research and teaching interests include political organizations, institutions, campaigns and elections, and religion and politics.

Politics and relations among individuals in societies across the world are being transformed by new technologies for targeting individuals and sophisticated methods for shaping personalized messages. The new technologies challenge boundaries of many kinds – between news, information, entertainment, and advertising; between media, with the arrival of the World Wide Web; and even between nations. *Communication, Society, and Politics* probes the political and social impacts of these new communication systems in national, comparative, and global perspective.

(Continued after the index)

Evaluating Campaign Quality

CAN THE ELECTORAL PROCESS BE IMPROVED?

L. Sandy Maisel
Colby College

Darrell M. West
Brown University

Brett M. Clifton
Brown University

CAMBRIDGE UNIVERSITY PRESS

CAMBRIDGE UNIVERSITY PRESS
Cambridge, New York, Melbourne, Madrid, Cape Town, Singapore, São Paulo

Cambridge University Press
32 Avenue of the Americas, New York, NY 10013-2473, USA

www.cambridge.org
Information on this title: www.cambridge.org/9780521877299

First published 2007

Printed in the United States of America

A catalog record for this publication is available from the British Library.

Library of Congress Cataloging in Publication Data

Maisel, Louis Sandy, 1945–
Evaluating campaign quality : can the electoral process be improved? /
L. Sandy Maisel, Darrell M. West, Brett M. Clifton.
p.   cm. – (Communication, society, and politics)
Includes bibliographical references and index.
ISBN-13: 978-0-521-87729-9 (hardback)
ISBN-13: 978-0-521-70082-5 (pbk.)
1. Political campaigns – United States.   2. Elections – United States.
I. West, Darrell M., 1954–   II. Clifton, Brett M., 1972–   III. Title.
JK2281.M35   2007
324.70973–dc22   2006101719

ISBN   978-0-521-87729-9 hardback
ISBN   978-0-521-70082-5 paperback

To William H. Goldfarb and
To A. Alfred Taubman and John Hazan White,
*with gratitude for their support over many years for us and the
institutions we serve*

Contents

Preface

This book analyzes whether campaign discourse and conduct can be improved through the reform of contemporary elections. For a number of years, voters and academic observers have been dissatisfied with a number of elements of American campaigns. Contemporary races are seen in several circles as too negative, too superficial, and too unfair or misleading. Based on these complaints, a variety of reform organizations have targeted millions of dollars to improve the situation.

Through their efforts and those within the academic community, a wide range of reform initiatives have been undertaken. Ideas such as voluntary codes of conduct, industry self-regulation, training schools, certificate programs, tougher ethics rules for consultants, and the encouragement of more substantive venues such as candidate debates, town meetings, and issue forums have been promulgated to improve the performance of American elections.

In this volume, we seek to evaluate whether these activities have improved the level of campaign discourse and conduct in U.S. House and Senate campaigns. Using a variety of information derived from a national public opinion survey, a survey of political consultants, focus groups, in-depth elite interviews, and a detailed content analysis of major campaign communications, we argue that while some reforms have improved campaigns, the overall impact has been disappointing. We suggest that this failure is due to a lack of understanding of the incentives facing campaign professionals. Reforms will not be successful unless they alter the incentives that candidates have to engage in bad behavior and avoid substantive discussion.

The outline of this book is as follows. In Chapter 1, we discuss how election observers are divided into three camps in their views about campaign reform. Optimists feel there are problems in the electoral process and support campaign changes they feel will address key weaknesses. Skeptics see problems with contemporary campaigns but believe they are endemic to the political process and therefore are not likely to be fixed through reform initiatives. Rejectionists believe larger forces such as war and peace and macroeconomic performance determine election results and that, as a result, campaign reform activities are not very influential in shaping public opinion or voting behavior. We discuss our view that campaigns are important and propose a method for evaluating the relationship between reform and campaign conduct. After reviewing indicators of reform success or failure, we present a typology of contemporary reforms that gauges the likely efficacy of different reform proposals.

In Chapter 2, we talk about the ways in which reforms relating to various campaign practices are disseminated among the attentive public. How visible are campaign reforms? To what extent were they implemented during recent congressional elections? We present the results of a campaign consultant survey and a national public opinion poll about reform activities in congressional races. Briefly, we find that consultants and voters were aware of reform proposals but did not evaluate most of them very positively.

Chapter 3 looks at candidate and consultant perceptions about campaign conduct. With efforts to clean up campaigns limited by court rulings and the inability of politicians to muster the courage to change the rules of the game, recent reforms have moved toward a focus on altering the behavior of campaign professionals, such as candidates and consultants. We discuss why many of these efforts have not been successful and why industry self-regulation is limited as a device for improving campaign quality. We present evidence from in-depth interviews, focus groups, and surveys of consultants in competitive districts and voters across the country to demonstrate why campaign reform efforts have not achieved their goals.

Chapter 4 examines candidate discourse through an independent study of actual campaign communications in the midterm election. What messages were conveyed through various media, such as advertisements, debates, mailings, and Web sites? One key focus of reformers has been in improving political discourse. By focusing on what candidates say, reformers aim to make campaigns more civil, less sullied, and more informative. However, our objective data from House and Senate races demonstrate that candidates have strong incentives to engage in negative and nonsubstantive campaign messages and that many proposed reforms failed to improve campaign conduct in these contests.

Chapter 5 looks at voter reactions to campaign reform proposals. Using a national public opinion survey, we examine whether voters felt favorable toward and saw meaningful results linked to campaign reform. In most cases, we found that voters were not aware of implemented reforms and did not link reform efforts to improvements in campaign conduct.

Chapter 6 argues that for political reform to be successful, it must be based on the incentives that drive candidates, consultants, reporters, and voters to behave in constructive ways. Some proposed reforms have failed because of an inadequate understanding of campaign incentives. We discuss the prospects for system-wide change emanating from campaign reform and outline several future changes that would improve American elections.

We have many debts of gratitude for this project. First, we are grateful to the Pew Charitable Trusts for funding our data collection. We have some of the most comprehensive data ever collected on the subject of campaign reform. We are especially grateful for the suggestions of Les Baxter, Laura Line, Michael Delli Carpini, Sean Treglia, and Rebecca Rimel. Their probing inquiries pushed us to refine our thoughts.

We are also grateful to the more than two dozen case study researchers who coded campaign communications in the most competitive U.S. House and Senate races in 2002. They are Bill Binning and Melanie Blumberg, Youngstown State University (OH-17); Chris Bratcher, Milsaps College (MS-3); Andrew Busch, Denver University (CO-7); Mark Brewer, University of Maine (ME Senate); Clyde Brown, Miami University of Ohio (OH-3); David Damore, University of Nevada (NV-3); Jay DeSart, Florida Atlantic University (FL-22); Todd Donovan, Western Washington University (WA-2); Marni Ezrta, Hood College (MD-8); Jose Garcia, New Mexico State University (NM-2); Dan Hofrenning, St. Olaf's College (MN Senate); John Jackson, Southern Illinois University (IL-19); Stephanie Larson, Dickinson College (PA-17); Burdett Loomis, Kansas University (KS-3); Cherie Maestas, Florida State University (TX Senate); Paul Manuel and Dante Scala, St. Anselm's University (NH-1); Kelly Patterson, Brigham Young University (UT-2); Paul Petterson, Central Connecticut State University (CT-2); Richard Powell, University of Maine (ME-2); Chuck Prysby, University of North Carolina, Greensboro (NC Senate); Maeve Reston, *Pittsburgh Post Gazette* (NH Senate); David Romero, University of Texas–San Antonio (TX-23); L. John Roos, University of Notre Dame (IN-2); Pat Sellers, Davidson University (NC-8); John Shockley, Augsburg College (MN-2); Fred Solop,

Northern Arizona University (AZ-1); and Jennifer Steen, Boston College (CT-5).

To help review all aspects of our research design, we relied on an Advisory Board, cochaired by Peter Hart and the late Robert Teeter. Hart and Teeter, among the nation's leading political pollsters, the former a Democrat and the latter a Republican, worked together on a number of bipartisan or nonpartisan projects. The remaining Board members are Douglas Bailey, who for many years was one of the leading Republican media consultants but who, most recently, has worked with Freedom's Answer, a nonprofit campaign in Washington working to increase voter participation among young voters; Marla Romash, of Romash Communications, a Democratic media firm; and John Simms, of Odell, Simms, and Associates, one of the leading Republican direct mail firms.

We also engaged a Peer Review Panel to oversee our research. That panel consisted of Anna Greenberg, vice president of Greenberg Quinlan Rosner Research, Inc., and former assistant professor of government at the John F. Kennedy School of Government, Harvard University; Larry Jacobs, professor of political science at the University of Minnesota; and Thomas E. Mann, Senior Fellow and holder of the W. Averill Harriman Chair in Governance Studies at the Brookings Institution. We owe a great debt to these scholars for their guidance throughout this work.

We want to thank Rhodes Cook, Stu Rothenberg, and Amy Walter for their assistance as we attempted to determine, months in advance of an election, which districts were most likely to see serious competition. Cherie Maestas was particularly helpful in the early stages of the content analysis, working on the development of the protocols and means for analysis. Sandy Maisel had outstanding research assistance from several undergraduates at Colby College: Brooke McNally, Laura Mistretta, and Abe Summers were very important throughout the project.

Finally, we are very grateful to Lew Bateman and Eric Crahan of Cambridge University Press and our two reviewers. These individuals had a number of suggestions that improved the organization, clarity, and presentation of our argument, and their comments made this a better book. None of these individuals or organizations bears any responsibility for the conclusions that we reach in this volume.

Portions of this manuscript were published in an article entitled "The Impact of Campaign Reform on Political Discourse," which appeared in *Political Science Quarterly* in its Winter 2005 issue. It is reprinted here with permission.

ONE

Campaign Reformers: Optimists, Skeptics, and Rejectionists

A t a time when much of the world is turning to democracy, it is ironic that many Americans are dissatisfied with the quality of their own political contests. Politicians are accused of adopting uncivil styles of discourse. Consultants are charged with engaging in manipulative and/or deceptive behavior. Observers say candidates avoid detailed substance in their campaign appeals. Voters complain that political campaigns have become overly negative and are not very informative.[1]

Given the dissatisfaction that exists regarding American campaigns, a broad range of academic writers and nongovernmental organizations has pushed for improvements in how races are conducted. Reform groups such as Common Cause, the Alliance for Better Campaigns, the Center for Voting and Democracy, the Institute for Global Ethics, and the Project for Excellence in Journalism have developed ideas for more debates and issue forums, providing training schools for consultants and journalists and strengthening ethical standards that they believe will improve the process. The Pew Charitable Trusts, the Markle Foundation, the Open Society Institute, the Ford Foundation, the Carnegie Corporation of New York, the Smith Richardson Foundation, and others have committed millions of dollars to investigating whether voluntary codes of conduct signed by candidates, self-regulation by consulting trade associations, the development of formal accreditation and certification programs for campaign consultants, and other reforms will strengthen democratic institutions.[2]

Despite the importance of these efforts, scholars have not engaged in a systematic evaluation of the propositions underlying these campaign reforms. Little research has examined the extent to which proposed reforms have been adopted or the reactions of the American public and campaign professionals to those that have been implemented. Where proposals have been adopted, there has been virtually no analysis to determine whether reforms are linked to intended improvements in candidate conduct and civil discourse.

In this book, we evaluate the work of those who have sought to improve the electoral process. We review alternative reform approaches based on the views of "optimists," "skeptics," and "rejectionists," categorizations that reflect differences in opinion regarding the nature of electoral problems and likely efficacy of proposed reforms. We do not seek to debunk the work of reformers but instead to apply rigorous theoretical and empirical analysis to their efforts. We believe that political science has important lessons to teach reformers. If their goal is to improve the system, we need a serious assessment to determine what changes can be implemented, given the institutional constraints that exist and the political incentives facing particular participants. What works and why does it succeed? What fails and why is it unsuccessful?

Using data from an in-depth content analysis of campaign communications, interviews with campaign professionals, a survey of campaign consultants active in competitive races, focus groups with campaigners, and a national public opinion survey, we investigate how campaign conduct is affected by reform efforts. We argue that while individual reform efforts have achieved some of their stated objectives, the overall effect of these reform efforts has been disappointing. To look at specific reforms that have been attempted, we find that voters appreciate debates and issue forums and pay attention to them during campaigns. But few candidates – particularly few in competitive races – have signed voluntary codes of conduct; consultants give little indication that they can regulate themselves or refrain from discourse that pushes the envelope in competitive contests. As we discuss in our concluding chapter, a different approach to improving campaign conduct and political discourse in American elections is clearly called for if improved campaigning is the goal.

DIFFERING VIEWS OF ELECTION PROBLEMS
AND THE VIABILITY OF CAMPAIGN REFORM

Political observers are divided in their views about the seriousness of electoral problems in the United States and the viability of proposed campaign reforms. In reviewing discussions about American elections, we find there are three general categories of electoral perspectives: rejectionist, optimist, and skeptical.

"Rejectionists" argue that elections are determined by government performance and that campaigns matter little in determining electoral outcomes. Following the classic tradition of V. O. Key, these scholars emphasize a reward/punishment model based on actual government indicators, such as the economy or war and peace.[3] If the economy (or a war) is going well and the public is satisfied with the overall performance of the current administration, they should vote for members of that administration's party; and if they are dissatisfied, they should punish the in-party by voting against its officials. As a consequence, these academics reject campaign reforms as unnecessary for the effective functioning of government.

This model of democracy requires only minimal information and choice on the part of the electorate. Voters are not required to follow policy debates very carefully or to research the details of a candidate's political platform. Rather, they simply must be able to judge whether the job is being performed by the current administration. Evaluating whether their personal standard of living is rising or declining, whether they have jobs, and whether they are satisfied or dissatisfied with the general course of affairs enables voters to compare competing candidates and hold political leaders accountable.[4]

Taken in this light, performance-based analysts tend to think that the quality of the campaign, the nature of candidate discourse, and the coverage by the mass media do not matter much in determining election results. Highly salient concerns (such as the unemployment rate, inflation, the number of troop fatalities, and the cost of gas prices) are what move voters.[5]

In contrast, "optimists" feel the campaign matters. With the weakening of party identifications and the tendency of voters to focus on short-term electoral factors, the quality of campaign discourse, the nature of candidate rhetoric, and the extent to which news coverage informs the public are critical at election time. It is not that government performance is irrelevant, but that high-quality campaign discourse and political communications are required to help voters hold officials accountable.[6] Democratic elections require healthy discourse, civil tones, and sufficient substance to enable voters to represent their interests. Deceitful or misleading candidate statements short-circuit democratic processes and weaken the accountability of the electoral process.[7]

According to this perspective, voters must be in a position to evaluate the degree to which incumbents are responsible for good or poor performance. Assessing blame is an inexact science and is an exercise in which many citizens need help. If they are interested in rewarding or punishing officials, citizens must pay some attention to political rhetoric and possess enough information to hold politicians accountable for general conditions. Citizens need effective campaigns and viable opposition leaders, not just platitudinous campaign rhetoric, in order to make these judgments effectively.

Unlike the rejectionists, optimists place great importance on the quality of the candidates and of their campaigns.[8] Voters not only have to decide among competing candidates, as is true with the first model, but they also have to be aware of policy alternatives, be able to judge the respective policy merits promulgated by different candidates, and hold leaders accountable for policy commitments. For such a system to work effectively, citizens must be very engaged in politics, have enough information to make up their minds on crucial matters, and ask tough questions of political leaders. This statement of democratic theory requires broader and more refined voter knowledge and political campaigns that convey substantive information to the public.

Given the importance of discourse and communications in democratic elections, optimists believe that the electoral process must be reformed to address key information deficiencies. Foremost among their list of complaints are the ideas that political campaigns have become non-substantive, deceptive, unfair, and overly negative in the information conveyed to the general public. According to a national opinion study, 39 percent of voters believe that all or most candidates deliberately lie to voters.[9]

In the eyes of some people, paid political consultants deserve blame for the poor quality of American campaigns. A national survey by the Pew Research Center found that 31 percent of Americans gave campaign consultants a grade of A or B, 29 percent gave them a C, and 13 percent rated their performance a D or F for the way they conducted themselves during the 2000 presidential election.[10] While there clearly is a division of opinion among the general public, 42 percent of Americans, a majority of those who had an opinion on this question, saw consultants performing at a C, D, or F level.

The public is unhappy with how reporters cover campaigns.[11] A majority of citizens (56 percent) argued that news stories often are inaccurate. This erosion of confidence in news-gathering has undermined public support for the press in general. During the course of the last two decades, the media's favorability ratings have dropped substantially.

Table 1-1. American Association of Political Consultants'
Code of Campaign Conduct

- I will not indulge in any activity which would corrupt or degrade the practice of political consulting.
- I will treat my colleagues and clients with respect and never intentionally injure their professional or personal reputations.
- I will respect the confidence of my clients and not reveal confidential or privileged information obtained during our professional relationship.
- I will use no appeal to voters which is based on racism, sexism, religious intolerance, or any form of unlawful discrimination and will condemn those who use such practices. In turn, I will work for equal voting rights and privileges for all citizens.
- I will refrain from false or misleading attacks on an opponent or member of his or her family and will do everything in my power to prevent others from using such tactics.
- I will document accurately and fully any criticism of an opponent or his or her record.
- I will be honest in my relationship with the news media and candidly answer questions when I have the authority to do so.
- I will use any funds I receive from my clients, or on behalf of my clients, only for those purposes invoiced in writing.
- I will not support any individual or organization which resorts to practices forbidden by this code.

Source: American Association of Political Consultants.

More and more citizens complain that reporters are biased, sensationalist, unfair, and inaccurate.[12]

The widespread and persistent nature of these complaints about the electoral process leads optimists to want to reform contemporary campaigns. With the extensive dissatisfaction that exists regarding American campaigns and elections, nongovernmental organizations and foundations concerned with good government have pushed for improvements in how American races are conducted.[13] As mentioned earlier, the specific reforms proposed cover a wide spectrum. To increase the substantive campaign content, some have suggested that candidates participate in more formal debates, forums, and town meetings; others have proposed that candidates be given free media time uninterrupted by press questioning.

Still other reformers have called for voluntary self-restraint on the part of candidates and consultants (see Table 1-1 for the American Association of Political Consultants' Code of Conduct). Campaign professionals have been urged to sign voluntary pledges in which they agree not to engage in campaigning that is unfair, deceptive, misleading, or overly negative.[14]

Others have recommended ethics codes for consultants that would penalize violators of agreed-upon professional standards; another group has designed training programs that teach candidates about campaign conduct. Finally, some have called for training programs run by universities or professional associations that would raise the level of ethics and professionalism within the consulting industry. As examples, the George Washington University has a school of campaign management, the University of California at Berkeley has a Center for Campaign Leadership, the University of Virginia has the Sorensen Institute for Political Leadership, and the University of Akron has the Bliss Institute of Applied Politics. All of these programs offer training and/or degree programs to improve campaign performance.

Election "skeptics" tend to agree that there are problems with contemporary campaigns; like the optimists but unlike the rejectionists, they believe that the campaigns matter. However, unlike the optimists, skeptics believe that many of the complaints about contemporary campaigns are endemic to the political process and are not likely to be fixed through reform initiatives.[15] For these individuals, criticisms about attacks, fairness, and superficial rhetoric represent the partisan, personal, and cyclical nature of politics. Depending on the nature of the political times, some elections are more substantive, while others are more superficial. Some feature more attacks, while others do not. These variations are merely part of the give and take of politics, not a cause for great alarm.[16]

If observers do not like the lack of specificity in candidate discussions or the tone of the rhetoric, it is a person's job in a democracy to criticize candidates on those bases. High-minded appeals to candidate self-restraint or enlightened political self-interest are not likely to be successful.[17] Politics is a participant activity, and reformers should not be "goody two shoes" who remain on the sidelines. They should engage with other partisans, fight fire with fire, and do all they can to defeat those who run campaigns with tactics they find repugnant.[18]

Skeptics believe that optimists do not understand office-seekers' political incentives. Some candidates will use whatever tactics are available to win elections – mean-spirited attacks, superficial rhetoric, or deceptive appeals – if the candidates and their advisors feel that those tactics will be successful in gaining more votes. According to the skeptics' viewpoint, the job of the candidates is to win votes by whatever legal means are at their disposal, not to stick to the issues nor to stay on the high road. Politics is a rough and tumble business, and optimists should not subject elections to unrealistic high-minded standards.

Samuel Popkin, a performance-based voting expert who is critical of reform optimists, states that there are valid grounds for questioning the hopefulness of electoral reformers. Political campaigns "are commonly criticized as tawdry and pointless affairs, full of dirty politics, dirty tricks, and mudslinging, which ought to be cleaned up, if not eliminated from the system.... Most suggestions for reforming the campaigns have no basis in any sustained argument about how proposed reforms would affect voters or improve the system."[19]

THE LOCUS OF OUR STUDY

Our goal in this project is not to evaluate every aspect of the reform agenda. Scholars have made proposals for change in a variety of different areas. Looking at presidential elections, some feel the Electoral College no longer serves the national interest.[20] Others want to strengthen political parties or rein in the high cost of contemporary campaigns.[21] Still others focus on the news media and the job they do in covering American races and how this affects citizen participation.[22] In light of irregularities in recent elections, another group focuses on ballot design and how particular features affect voting.[23]

Our goal is to establish criteria and then to evaluate an important set of reforms, not to propose new ideas. We seek to evaluate campaign discourse and conduct in House and Senate campaigns in order to ascertain whether particular reforms are associated with real or perceived improvements in elections.[24] We do not accept the rejectionists' view that campaigns do not matter. Even if government performance is the major determinant of voting behavior, the quality of the campaign and the nature of the political communications make a difference. Unless voters have help in judging candidates, it is difficult for them to represent their self-interest and hold government officials accountable. But we do not accept the optimists' view either. Reform for reform sake should not be the goal. We believe that reformers must have specific goals in mind and that reform efforts should be evaluated against those goals. However, we do not fall into the skeptics' camp either. We want to evaluate specific reforms and determine why they do or do not work before we are ready to conclude that effective reform is or is not possible.

In the debate between optimists and skeptics, we are not sure who is right in their interpretation of reform efficacy. Both perspectives agree that the campaign matters, but one side thinks reform will be effective, while the other side tends to believe politics will trump reform at the end of the day. Ultimately, we believe that whether those ideas that have been implemented in congressional races have produced the benefits envisioned by optimists is an empirical question. We further believe that understanding why they have or have not been effective is critical to evaluating the possibility of fundamental change.

To that end, in this study, we focus on campaign discourse and conduct because they have been central to reform organization activities and are key to democratic representation and accountability. It is an empirical matter whether districts where candidates have taken a pledge to avoid negative campaigning have produced campaigns that are more civil and more informative than places where such pledges have not been made. In the same vein, we focus on campaign conduct because the behavior of campaign participants, such as candidates and consultants, is vital to how citizens view the political process. Do districts where campaigners have engaged in practices defined by reform advocates as misleading or unethical exhibit campaign conduct that is different from that found elsewhere? Our task in the remainder of this volume is to see to what extent these efforts have been successful in improving American elections.

Our locus of study of electoral reform is campaign discourse and conduct in the context of the 2002 House and Senate elections. We emphasize House and Senate campaigns because they have been central to public concerns about elections. Legislative races have engendered many complaints about one-sided races, nasty rhetoric, weak media coverage, and unethical tactics. As such, they constitute a meaningful vehicle for evaluating campaign reform efforts.

Midterm elections also offer the advantage of a pure look at congressional races without the distraction of a presidential campaign. Presidential campaign races attract much more media and scholarly attention than do congressional races, which make the latter an important object of scholarly study. Since House and Senate midterm elections are crucial to policymaking and are not contaminated with presidential election effects, they represent a valuable opportunity to study the impact of campaign reform on discourse and conduct.

The 2002 election was noteworthy because it featured an agenda that was balanced between foreign policy and traditional domestic concerns such as the economy, health care, taxes, and education. This campaign was also the first national election following the September 11, 2001, terrorist attacks on New York City and Washington, DC. As such, it allows us to see how a dramatic external attack affected styles of campaigning in midterm elections.

In focusing on campaign discourse and conduct, we are not denigrating efforts to improve political parties, campaign finance, ballot structures, redistricting, or other kinds of political reform.[25] Each of these foci is vitally important to the health of American democracy. One cannot have democratic elections without strong parties, fair campaign finance rules, districts that are drawn in a manner to foster possible competition, and ballots that are understandable to ordinary citizens.

Yet we argue that there also needs to be attention to the concerted efforts that have been made to improve the quality of campaign discourse and conduct in the United States. These are areas that have been the object of sustained time, energy, and money on the part of foundations, interest groups, universities, and nonprofit organizations. As students of the political process, we need to determine to what extent these activities have been effective.

INDICATORS OF REFORM SUCCESS OR FAILURE

To determine whether reform has been successful in regard to campaign discourse and conduct, we developed a variety of methodologies and indicators of how electoral reform affects the quality of campaigns. One of the things we discovered in undertaking this study is that there are no widely accepted models of effective discourse and quality conduct. Some researchers focus more on the problem of poor-quality information provided by media reporters, while others emphasize issues posed by candidate deception and manipulation. Still others point out the power of special interest groups in skewing campaign discourse, while other scholars complain that voters are not engaged in the political process and are not very informed about their campaign choices. Certainly many are concerned with the lack of civility in the ways in which candidates communicate with and about one another.

In addition, there is disagreement over how deleterious particular discourse problems are.[26] For example, some writers complain that "negative" advertising depresses voter interest and engagement while many others have disputed those results. Some see reporters playing legitimate roles in policing ads and serving as referees for campaign discourse, while others believe journalists are ill-equipped to engage in that type of oversight.

In this study, we look at discourse and conduct in House and Senate races. Using more than two dozen academic experts (acknowledged in the Preface), we undertook a detailed quantitative content analysis of ads, news, debates, mailings, and candidate Web sites in the races we deemed most competitive some months before the election, when this research commenced. Among other things, our local academic experts in each area coded communications for issue content, bias, tone, cognitive versus emotional appeal, character information, specificity, and the object of negativity.

Our assessment of candidate discourse followed from several qualities of effective elections that are widely accepted by reform advocacy organizations and "optimistic" academic reformers. Leaders in reform organizations believe that electoral discourse should be substantive, not overly negative, unbiased, and not misleading or deceptive. Therefore, our independent experts studied campaign communications to see what the degree of issue content, bias, and tone was and whether there were any differences between districts (or states) where reforms were adopted versus places where they were not. Presumably, if a congressional district had debates, issue forums, or pledges to avoid negativity, there should be improved discourse and conduct if reform prescriptions are to be considered effective.

The rationale reformers have for wanting substantive communications is that if voters have a choice, they must understand that choice. That is, the substance of campaign discourse must make clear to the voters what distinguishes one candidate from another based on experience, past record, proven ability, positions on the issues, the ability to accomplish goals, or a number of other relevant factors. Candidates need to convey this information to voters in a way that gets through to them and is not too shrill or negative because those types of tactics turn off many voters and may discourage them from participating in the electoral process. Discourse that is biased, misleading, deceptive, or unfair is thought to complicate the voter's task of holding leaders accountable and representing citizen interests in the political process.[27]

These requirements have led many reform organizations to focus on candidate discourse and patterns of media coverage as key measures of campaign quality. From their standpoint, a "good" campaign involves substantive campaigns that present options to voters in a way that allows them to vote for candidates with whom they agree on fundamental matters (i.e., issues, traits, values, or backgrounds). Citizens should have the opportunity to know where candidates stand on the issues, what qualifications they would bring to the office, how they would represent the district – each of these in concrete terms, not in meaningless platitudes.

Furthermore, following the lead of reform organizations, we were concerned about the civility and tone of the discourse. In looking for civility, we were acutely aware of the need for precise definitions. Candidates have become quite adept at crying "foul" when opponents use negative tactics against them. The media often pick up on these claims. However, contrasting one's record with that of one's opponent is a perfectly legitimate tactic for drawing exactly the type of distinction that citizens need to see in order to cast informed votes. Contrast or comparison ads are not necessarily negative, particularly if they are done objectively or with humor or subtlety. Therefore, we distinguish positive ads (in which a candidate sought support by emphasizing his or her own positive qualities or record), comparison or contrast advertising (in which a candidate explicitly compared his or her record with that of the opponent), and negative advertising (in which the clear goal of the candidate was to paint an unflattering picture of the opponent, without comparison to the person mounting the campaign).

Another set of indicators concerned the dissemination, visibility, and awareness of reform. We commissioned two telephone surveys designed to measure the visibility of reform among campaign consultants active in the most competitive campaigns and among voters across the country. Right after the 2002 election, Peter Hart and the late Robert Teeter undertook two national surveys – one of 197 campaign consultants active in the most competitive House and Senate campaigns in that election and a second of 642 American voters randomly selected throughout the nation. The consultant survey was conducted from November 6 to 25, 2002, and had a margin of error of plus or minus seven percentage points. The voter survey was undertaken from November 8 to 11, 2002, with a margin of error of plus or minus five percentage points.

If voters or campaign consultants see little evidence of campaign reform in their districts or do not see a tie between reform and improved conduct and discourse, the argument of the optimists that reform will reduce corruption (or the perception thereof) from the electoral process and help restore citizen faith in government is undermined.[28] Many reform organizations have taken as their goal restoring public confidence in government and reversing the high levels of mistrust that have arisen over the past few decades in American politics. We wanted to see how widely various reforms such as debates, issue forums, codes of conduct, and training schools have disseminated across the country and whether consultants or voters saw evidence of these efforts in House districts and Senate races.

In addition to examining campaign discourse in competitive races and looking at the visibility of campaign reform, we employed a quasi-experimental research design in which we compared campaign discourse in 27 of the most competitive congressional races in 2002. In five contests, candidates signed a voluntary code of conduct pledge developed by a national reform organization, the Institute for Global Ethics, while in 22, there were no formal pledges to avoid negative, misleading, or deceptive campaign appeals. Using our content analysis of ads, news, debates, and other forms of political communication, we evaluated whether campaigns in which this particular reform was adopted featured discourse that was more positive, more substantive, and less biased than districts where no reforms were present.

By comparing districts with targeted reform activities to areas with no reforms and contrasting campaigns where pledges to avoid campaign negativity were signed by candidates with those where they were not, our goal was to make a specific comparison of the impact of reform on political discourse. If reforms are effective, one would expect districts having debates, no-negative-ad pledges, and other types of reform activities to feature discourse that is more substantive and less negative in tone.

Finally, we undertook a multivariate assessment of the determinants of campaign quality. Relying on our content analysis data, we looked at a variety of factors important in election campaigns that potentially could affect campaign discourse. These include variables such as the party of the candidate, whether an incumbent is running or the seat is open, whether a candidate or noncandidate sponsored the communication, whether the candidate personally appeared in the communication, and whether the appeal relied on emotion or cognition. We used this analysis to assess the factors that either encourage or discourage higher quality campaign discourse to take place.

A TYPOLOGY OF CONTEMPORARY REFORMS

In thinking of the possible impact of contemporary reforms, it is clear that not all changes are of the same ilk. Contemporary reforms can be classified into several variants, based on how visible and understandable the reform is to voters. As shown in Table 1-2, reforms can be either easy or hard to understand, depending on how much effort it takes for voters to decipher them, and either visible or invisible to voters during the campaign. Debates, town meetings, and free television time for candidates

Table 1-2. Typology of Campaign Conduct Reforms

Voter Ability to Understand	Campaign Visibility	
	Visible	Invisible
Easy to understand	Debates; issue forums; town meetings; free television time	None
Hard to understand	Candidate pledges on campaign conduct and negativity; media ad watches	Consultant/journalist training programs; consultant ethics codes; accreditation programs; certification programs

are relatively easy to understand from the citizens' standpoint because these are communications vehicles where voters can watch (or read) and make up their own minds about the candidates.

Other reforms, in contrast, are harder to grasp; some seek to improve the campaign process indirectly while others force voters to make assumptions about the campaigns that are less clear. The Institute for Global Ethics and others have proposed self-restraint on the part of candidates and consultants, asking campaign professionals to sign pledges voluntarily agreeing not to engage in campaigning that is unfair, deceptive, misleading, or overly negative. Pledge signings are often publicized by both the candidates and the media.

Some reformers have proposed training programs (some accredited or in the form of a certificate program) for campaign consultants and journalists, respectively, that would professionalize each industry and provide examples of "best practices" that would improve campaign conduct. Still other organizations have suggested ethics codes for consultants that would penalize violators of agreed-upon professional standards. These ethics codes would be administered by professional organizations, such as the American Association of Political Consultants, the major trade association of consultants. Each of these reforms seeks to improve campaign discourse indirectly, through changing the actions of those who are determining campaign messages. But these reforms are inherently harder for voters to grasp than more direct and straightforward reforms such as holding open debates among the candidates.

In analyzing reforms, some are visible during the campaign while others are invisible. Debates, town meetings, and conduct pledges are part of the campaign, visible to voters, and have the potential to alter citizen impressions of the candidates. Others, such as campaign training schools, journalist training programs, consultant ethics codes, program accreditation, and certification programs, are more behind the scenes during the campaign and less visible to voters, and therefore are less direct in their possible impact on voters.

We hypothesize in this book that the success of proposed reforms depends in part on the qualities of the specific reform. Campaign reforms that are most likely to be successful in improving campaign conduct are those that are visible, direct, and understandable. If voters have an easy time seeking to understand a particular reform and the reform is visible to them during the campaign, those activities have the greatest potential (real or perceived) to be effective at improving campaigns.

In contrast, reforms that are hard to grasp, indirect, and/or invisible to voters during the campaign are least likely to be effective. If voters do not understand reforms or see evidence of their presence during the campaign, candidates can more easily manipulate the reforms to their own advantage. For example, in the case of "no negativity" pledges or signing codes of conduct, it is easy for candidates to obfuscate bad conduct and blame their opponents (or the media) for questionable tactics during the election. This confuses voters and short-circuits the opportunity for democratic accountability.

By looking at different types of reforms, our goal in this volume is to determine whether the electoral process can be improved and what specific changes would make campaign discourse and conduct better. It is important to look at various reforms to see which ones are associated with more substantive discussion, more civil discourse, fairer appeals, and less negative campaigning. If voters are to become less cynical about the political process, they need campaigns that help them make fundamental electoral choices.

TWO

Dissemination of Campaign Practices

Reformers can propose wonderful ideas about improving electoral campaigns, but if these suggestions are not disseminated, visible to voters and campaign participants, and if they do not have a discernible impact on campaign discourse and conduct, they are not very effective. Candidates and political consultants must be made aware of campaign reforms because they are the ones who make decisions on going negative and the degree of substantive appeals to incorporate into campaign communications.

At a point when campaigns have become professional, organized entities with multimillion dollar budgets, the views and behavior of consultants are crucial. Their opinions matter because their impressions of the political climate, media reaction, and possible backlash against particular tactics influence their behavior. If they believe that reporters and citizens will punish unfair tactics, vague discourse, or harsh attacks on the opposition, they will be far less likely to employ these strategies than if they perceive few risks to those kinds of behaviors.

At the same time, voters represent an important audience for political reforms. Citizens are the ones who remain deeply cynical about contemporary campaigns. After witnessing unsatisfactory government performance and shrill campaigns featuring misleading or unfair communications, average citizens see politicians as failing to serve societal interests or the common good. Rather, these candidates are seen as advancing their own parochial interests.

In this chapter, we examine consultant and voter impressions of House and Senate contests. Using national surveys of voters and consultants who were active in the most competitive races that year, as well as in-depth interviews and focus groups with leading consultants, we explore the extent to which "good" campaign practices (as defined by reform organizations) are disseminated across the country. Were consultants and voters aware of proposed reforms? How did campaign professionals and voters evaluate these suggestions for change?

After examining the survey, interview, and focus group results, we found that reform information was available and disseminated to a broad audience of voters and consultants. However, the amount of visibility and degree of implementation varied substantially among the reforms. Simple reforms that were easy to understand disseminated much more broadly than complex reforms involving codes of conduct and pledges not to engage in negative campaigning. Political professionals fell into the skeptic camp with regard to the latter reforms because they did not see them altering campaign conduct in a meaningful way, undermining the position of reform optimists regarding the efficacy of suggested changes.

THE VIEWS OF CONSULTANTS

A number of nonpartisan organizations have undertaken serious efforts to improve campaign discourse and conduct in the United States. They organized seminars for campaign participants on ethical campaigning. They sought to get candidates to sign voluntary codes of conduct pledging to avoid negative, misleading, or unfair campaign practices. They encouraged local groups to sponsor debates and issue forums with the goal that more substantive discussion would take place in these venues.

In undertaking these activities, these groups attempted to improve the substance, tone, and civility of congressional races. Their assumptions in pushing for these types of changes was that democratic elections need some degree of substance for effective representation and accountability, and that fair conduct and respect for the rules of the game are helpful for voters to make choices among competing candidates.

Some of the proposed reforms, such as debates and issue forums, have been around for a long time. Ever since John Kennedy and Richard Nixon debated on national television in 1960 and Jimmy Carter and Gerald Ford resumed the presidential debate practice in 1976, civic groups have sought to increase the frequency of candidate debates. The thinking is that in a one-on-one encounter between opposing candidates, voters have the best chance for substantive, civil, and fair discourse. Candidates find it more difficult to attack their opponents unfairly when directly confronting someone who has the opportunity to defend himself or herself. Furthermore, debates encourage detailed exchanges on the issues because they typically last at least one hour and cover a range of substantive matters.

Indeed, research on the 1976 election shows that debates tend to be more substantive than news coverage or paid advertisements. "The 1976 presidential debates produced a better informed electorate than would have been the case without them," according to political scientists Arthur Miller and Michael MacKuen.[1] Not only did the debates boost political awareness, they also increased policy knowledge and information about candidate qualities.

These conclusions are mirrored with regard to races below the presidential level. Debates and issue forums feature more substantive information than ads or the news because there is more time and they represent a format that encourages deeper policy discussions. In addition, with renewed media attention to fact-checking, candidates stick closely to factual information in highly visible settings, fearing they will be accused of engaging in unfair or misleading campaign appeals were they not to do so.

Other ideas, such as conduct codes or pledges to avoid negativity, are relatively recent additions to the reform agenda. These ideas were encouraged by foundations, academics, and nonpartisan observers as a way to improve the civility of contemporary campaigns. With concern that excessive negativity would depress voter turnout, reformers sought to increase voter interest by restraining the level of negativity in campaign discourse.

Shortly after the 2002 election, we surveyed consultants who were active in the most competitive U.S. House and Senate races across the country.[2] In this survey, we asked campaign managers, pollsters, media advisors, direct mail specialists, and general strategists whether various ideas designed to improve the tone and content of election campaigns were present in the congressional races in which they were involved. Ninety-one percent of consultants said there were formal candidate debates in the campaign in which they participated, 82 percent indicated there were issue forums where both candidates appeared, 41 percent said their staff or candidate attended a campaign training school, 29 percent noted that at least one of the candidates in their races pledged to avoid negative campaigning, and 25 percent said that at least one of the congressional candidates pledged to abide by a specific code of conduct in running their campaigns.

These numbers fit the general model we have sketched out in this book. Some reforms, such as debates and forums, have achieved high visibility and awareness among campaign professionals, while others, such as conduct pledges, have not. As we illustrate later in this volume, this disparity in reform visibility has ramifications for which changes are associated with improvements in discourse and conduct. Campaign professionals take invisible reforms less seriously and view them as less efficacious than more visible activities.

Among the organizations seeking to improve American elections was the nonpartisan Institute for Global Ethics (IGE), a project funded by the Pew Charitable Trusts. The goal of the IGE project was to get candidates for federal office to sign a voluntary code of conduct pledging to run their campaigns with high ethical standards and to refrain from negative, attack-oriented campaign strategies. Pew funded several similar grants to universities and nonprofit groups designed to spread this idea across the country and get congressional candidates to sign a formal pledge.

However, when asked if they had heard of this IGE reform activity involving code of conduct pledges, nearly two-thirds of the consultants (65 percent) responded negatively. This limited awareness clearly complicates the task of affecting the campaign process in the manner desired by reformers.

Of consultants who said they had heard of the IGE reform effort, only 17 percent indicated their own candidate had taken this pledge to abide by a voluntary code of conduct and 12 percent said the opposing candidate had taken the pledge. Fifty-five percent of political consultants whose candidates took the pledge claimed they lived up to the pledge very well, compared to 18 percent who said they did fairly well, 18 percent who believed their performance was just somewhat acceptable, and 9 percent who indicated they had not performed very well on the pledge. When asked their view of the impact of the pledge on the overall tone of the campaign, 82 percent said it had not had much of an effect, 9 percent claimed it had a fairly big effect, and 9 percent believed it had somewhat of an effect on campaign tone.

These findings suggest that it was easier for direct and straightforward reforms, such as debates and issue forums, to gain visibility and have a perceived impact. More complex reforms, such as pledges to avoid negativity and conduct codes, attract less attention, are manipulable by candidates, and are relatively invisible to voters. Based on the perceptions of campaign consultants, these constraints limit their ability to produce meaningful changes in the political process.

We also looked at how campaign participants felt about the ability of proposed reforms to improve campaign discourse and conduct. By examining perceptions of effect, we gauge how consultants think about the potential for particular reforms to make a positive difference in the electoral process. If campaign professionals are not optimistic about reform improving the process, it does not necessarily mean such reforms will be ineffective. Reforms can produce significant changes in discourse and conduct even if participants are doubtful of those things happening. But it is important to assess their viewpoint in order to determine what they saw taking place in congressional contests.

Indeed, many consultants surveyed are dubious about the potential of voluntary codes of conduct to make a meaningful difference in the campaign. Nearly half (48 percent) believed that pledges including a promise not to appeal to voters based on racism, sexism, religious intolerance, or other unlawful forms of discrimination, to refrain from false or misleading attacks on opponents, to document criticisms of an opponent's record, and to be honest and candid in dealing with the news media were not very effective in improving campaign behavior. Thirty-nine percent, however, thought such a code of conduct would be somewhat effective, while 7 percent believed it would be fairly effective, and 4 percent indicated it would be very effective.

Among those who felt voluntary codes of conduct would be effective, the top reasons given for this stance were that the idea had a lot of potential (17 percent), that their campaign had been open and honest in documenting the record (13 percent), that negative campaigning does not work (9 percent), that such reforms would force candidates to document everything (9 percent), that pledges make candidates run more ethical campaigns (7 percent), that more people would vote (7 percent), and that voters would get a more accurate reading of a candidate's record (7 percent).

Consultants who did not believe that codes of conduct would be effective gave a number of reasons for this impression. Among them were the belief that such codes were not effective and would not work (17 percent), that winning is the most important thing in a campaign (15 percent), that pledges would not stop candidates from engaging in such tactics (9 percent), that a code would be effective only if both sides abide by it (9 percent), that negative campaigning works (6 percent), that enforcement problems exist (6 percent), that the media would have to do a better job of informing the public when candidates honor the pledge (6 percent), that it goes too far in restricting candidates (5 percent), that it is not realistic (5 percent), and that no enforcement and no accountability occurs (5 percent).

We undertook in-depth interviews and focus group conversations with industry leaders in the consulting profession to see why they thought reformers' efforts would not be effective. They cited several reasons for their doubts. The main obstacle is that candidates run to win and consultants seek to make money. One individual said that candidates are "consumed by winning" and would do whatever it took to gain victory, including engaging in mudslinging or using dubious tactics. Consultants have monetary incentives tied to election victories that encourage them to test electoral limits.

In a separate American University survey of political consultants, for example, making money was the second most common reason given for becoming a professional consultant (after political beliefs and ideology).[3] Since consultants make more money if they run winning campaigns, they will do whatever helps their candidate win. Candidates sometimes are explicit about what they will and will not do in order to win, but few draw rigid lines for their consultants. Media and general consultants seem to feel that the tone of campaigns would change only when the public demands it. Candidates and consultants will set a positive tone for a campaign when they think that is what the public wants to hear.

Many of those interviewed argued with academic or press definitions of negative campaigning. When given similar scenarios, some consultants dubbed them as negative, some negative but ethical, and some perfectly appropriate "contrast" ads. Indeed, one participant described a contrast ad as "a polite way of edging into negative." One common theme was that no consultant would say that he or she has ever run a campaign in an unethical manner, but most would say that at least one of their opponents had done so. Similarly, consultants generally believe that contrast ads, deemed negative by some, are not only ethical, but are also the most effective way of giving the electorate grounds to make sound judgments. However, consultants disagreed on the extent to which positions could be exaggerated or taken out of context. Some claimed such actions were unethical, while others said that exaggerating positions was exactly how citizens had the best chance to see true differences.

Many of the leading consultants we talked to argued that pledges to avoid negative campaigning were not very effective in improving American elections. Indeed, some laughed and said a pledge to avoid attacks on the opposition was a wonderful idea for helping incumbents to protect their seats against challengers: "You're unknown and have no money and I have a lot of money. That's a great idea." Without challengers being able to confront incumbents about their records, consultants argued such pledges would make it easier for incumbents to win reelection. Some suggested that their candidates would sign such pledges because they would be considered "meaningless" in any case. For much the same reason, others indicated they would advise against signing any sort of pledge.

When asked what ethical standards guided their profession, the consultants invoked a variation of Justice Potter Stewart's famous line about pornography. They do not know how to describe the standards, but they know them when they see them. In the ensuing discussion, some consultants pointed out that campaign claims must be based on facts, but others noted that consultants play fast and loose with that ethical line and that a "facts" line is self-imposed and self-interpreted by each individual. One participant described the ethical line as "really whatever people can get away with without feeling sort of legally vulnerable or exposed."

Improved media oversight is another way reformers have sought to enhance campaign conduct. Ad watches, which provide press oversight of the accuracy of commercials, were cited in our focus groups as making candidates "hugely careful now." By encouraging journalists to devote more attention to politics and campaign coverage, the press can act as a check on unfair candidate tactics.[4] At the presidential level, for example, participants indicated that a misstep "is going to be covered in a lot, much higher degree of intensity." This helps to improve the tone and substance of political campaigns.

However, consultants were not convinced that media watches proved to be a meaningful way to improve campaign communications. Only 22 percent said that they thought ad watches had a great deal of effect in making campaigns more careful about ad content, while 24 percent thought they had a fair effect, 27 percent believed there was just some effect, 15 percent felt there was not much effect, and 10 percent thought there was no effect at all.

The general skepticism expressed by consultants suggests that serious barriers exist to some types of reforms being very effective. The greatest skepticism took place in regard to proposals such as conduct codes and pledges to avoid negativity. These reforms were seen as ineffective and subject to candidate manipulation. They also were viewed as a major obstacle to congressional challengers who wished to unseat incumbents having much higher recognition and funding.

While individual consultants might engage in "roguish" and unethical behavior, the hope of reformers is that in the long run, professional associations pushing for improved training will encourage campaign professionals to engage in better conduct. By upgrading the industry, the goal is that down the road, the manner in which electoral campaigns are conducted will be improved.

This idea is not unique to the world of political consulting. In the medical and legal professions, the idea is that industry self-regulation is an effective way to train people about better performance. Professional associations can penalize bad behavior. By acting as an oversight agent, the worst abuses can be publicized and their perpetrators reprimanded, to the betterment of the entire business.[5]

For these reasons, some reformers have focused on the American Association of Political Consultants (AAPC), the Washington-based major association of those consulting in politics, to clean up consulting abuses. The organization has a code of ethics and an ethics committee empowered to sanction unethical behavior. It also sponsors training programs designed to professionalize the industry.

However, only 22 percent of the consultants in our survey of the consultants involved in the most hotly contested elections said they were members of the AAPC; 78 percent were not (see Table 2-1).[6] It obviously is difficult to justify a strategy relying on AAPC enforcement when so few of the major consultants in the most competitive races are association members.

Even more problematic, most consultants surveyed, including many of those who were members of the AAPC, were not aware that the AAPC had a code of ethics. Thirty-five percent said they had never heard of it, 28 percent had but were not familiar with it, 17 percent indicated they were somewhat familiar with it, 10 percent said they were fairly familiar with it, and 10 percent stated they were very familiar with it.

Of those who were familiar with the AAPC's ethics code, 69 percent described it as a formality that did not have much practical application, while 17 percent thought it was a serious and important pledge. Asked to rate its effect on their consulting peers, 25 percent said the ethics code had no effect at all, 36 percent described the impact as not very much, 25 percent indicated it had just some effect, 5 percent believed it had a fair amount, and 2 percent thought it had a great deal of effect on consultant behavior.

Our survey asked consultants to rate the impact of the AAPC ethics code on their own behavior. Twenty-three percent said it had no effect at all, 23 percent believed the impact was not very much, 17 percent said it had some effect, 17 percent described the impact as a fair amount, and

Table 2-1. Professional Association Involvements
of Campaign Consultants

Members of AAPC	22
aware of AAPC ethics code	
never heard of it	35
heard of it but not familiar with it	28
somewhat familiar with it	17
fairly familiar	10
very familiar	10
Perception of AAPC ethics code effect on consulting peers	
no effect	25
not very much	36
some effect	25
fair amount	5
great deal of effect	2
Perception of AAPC ethics code effect on themselves	
no effect	23
not very much	23
some effect	17
fair amount	17
great deal of effect	9

Values represent percentages.
Source: Campaign Consultant Survey, November 2002.

9 percent rated the effect as having a great deal of impact on consultant actions.

Moreover, the industry leaders we interviewed were unanimous in agreeing that credentialing or licensing through the AAPC was an ineffective idea. They felt that a tough industry code of ethics, administered through the AAPC, was a nonstarter. Their reasons varied. Some felt that the industry did not require the same kinds of expertise as did lawyering or doctoring, so no licensing test was possible. Others claimed that definitions of what were ethical and unethical tactics, with few exceptions, were indefinable (and that no reputable consultant engaged in those clearly deemed unethical). Most claimed that the AAPC was ill suited for the task, that it was a trade organization set up to work *for* the industry, not to police it.

A number of the industry leaders we talked to were AAPC Board members who believed in the organization, but they did not feel rules enforcement was an appropriate role for the organization. A number of others were members who said they would resign if the AAPC moved in this direction. Still others, again for a variety of reasons, were not members and had no intention of joining.

A crucial aspect of the self-regulation model is whether industry organizations can monitor and impose sanctions on members who violate professional standards. The American Association for Public Opinion Research, for example, attracted national publicity in 1997 when it censured GOP pollster Frank Luntz for refusing to disclose question wording and survey results regarding his 1994 claim that 60 percent of the American public supported each provision of the Republican "Contract with America." Even though Luntz was not a member of that organization, the group's board voted to censure him because it thought he had acted in an unprofessional way that brought disrepute onto the polling industry.[7]

In our survey of consultants, we asked whether a professional organization such as the AAPC should be able to censure those who violate a code of ethics for campaign professionals. Forty-eight percent said yes, 39 percent argued against such a proposition, and 13 percent were unsure, demonstrating how controversial such an action would be for a professional association to undertake against someone in their own area.

Another way in which the AAPC could improve the professional climate of their industry is through training programs. Training programs could be in the form of activities that the association organizes itself or instruction undertaken in conjunction with university campaign management programs. However, when we asked consultants whether they would favor proposals that the AAPC develop a certificate training program for campaign professionals that would emphasize high standards in campaign practices, 34 percent believed this would not be very useful, 35 percent thought it would be somewhat helpful, and only 14 percent described such a program as fairly helpful and 15 percent as very useful.

Thus, one cannot find much potential for an industry self-regulation model.[8] The fact that most consultants are not members of the AAPC limits the ability of the organization to be effective. In addition, there appears to be little support for this professional association to take a more aggressive role. Indeed, most members were not even aware that the organization had an ethics code. Unlike the medical or legal professions, which are hierarchical and have clear entry points into the profession, anyone can claim to be a campaign consultant and launch a business. The openness of the profession makes it very difficult for self-regulation or for an association to impose meaningful sanctions on members. The industry simply is not well developed enough to take on this type of responsibility.

Consultants feel that the political consulting business is quite different from business or corporate consulting. For example, they noted that, unlike the corporate world, there is only one day in the election business for the product (a candidate) to be bought. Candidates need distinctive and highly targeted messages. Winning is everything because the day after the election, the loser goes out of business. Since making money is the ultimate goal of many consultants, it is vital to have some wins under their belts in order to be able to recruit future candidates. Reforms that do not address this fundamental motivation are not likely to be successful.

The last set of consultant perceptions we examined concerned views about the overall campaign. One of the goals of reformers is to change perceptions about the campaign process. To ascertain if progress had been made toward this goal, we asked how participants saw the quality of campaign tone and issue specificity. We used three questions to evaluate discourse: (1) Thinking for a moment about the 2002 general election cycle overall, not just this race, do you think that this year's campaign was generally more positive, generally more negative, or had about the same tone as recent election cycles? (2) And again, thinking about the 2002 general election cycle overall, would you say that there was more discussion of policy issues this year, less discussion of issues this year, or about the same amount of discussion as in past election cycles? And (3) do you feel that the campaign ads that ran in your race were generally helpful, added to voters' ability to understand the positions and qualifications of the two candidates, and helped the election process, or do you feel that the ads were not helpful, were just aimed at providing negative information about the opponent, and hurt the election process?

Unfortunately, consultants are not very sanguine about the style or substance of the midterm campaign. As shown in Table 2-2, consultants believed that the general election was more negative in tone than previous elections (40 percent) while far fewer (11 percent) found it more positive; 49 percent felt the tone was about the same as recent election cycles. Thirty-two percent believed there was less discussion of policy issues, 11 percent felt there was more discussion, and 57 percent said there was about the same amount of policy discussion as in past election cycles.

Although consultants' tendency to deny that any of their own ads were negative but that many of their opponents' advertisements were negative is well established, consultants were more likely to believe that less than half rather than more than half of their opponents' ads were negative.

Table 2-2. Consultant Feelings
About the Campaign

Tone of campaign	
negative	40
positive	14
Level of discussion	
less policy discussion	32
more policy discussion	11
Value of ads to voters	
ads helpful	51
ads hurtful	22

Values represent percentages.
Source: Campaign Consultant Survey, November 2002.

Thirty percent said that only a quarter or less of their opponent's ads were negative, 32 percent thought that somewhere between one-quarter and one-half were negative, 23 percent believed that something between one-half and three-quarters were negative, and 10 percent felt that more than three-quarters of the ads were negative in tone.

Of course, congressional campaigns leave much of the negative campaigning to surrogates and independent groups. This view was confirmed by our survey respondents who thought that many more of the independent advertisements were negative in tone. Thirty percent believed that at least three-quarters of the independent ads were negative, while 15 percent felt that somewhere between one-half and three-quarters were negative, 14 percent believed something between one-quarter and one-half were negative, and 24 percent believed that less than a quarter of the independent ads were negative. As others have noted, it is hard to police candidate ads when those that outside groups run are the most negative, deceptive, and misleading advertisements.[9]

THE VIEWS OF VOTERS

In addition to looking at the impressions of campaign professionals, we sought to gauge the views of voters across the country. In a separate survey, we polled a national sample of 642 voters.[10] Our voter sample focused on races across the country because we felt it was important to see how a national cross section of American voters felt about the election and the role of reform activities.

In general, we found low visibility among citizens in regard to reform efforts. Only 46 percent were aware of debates in their local congressional district, while 44 percent were aware of issue forums. This is much lower than the figures reported by consultants in competitive races. Of course, most congressional elections are not very competitive, and uncompetitive races typically do not generate as many debates and forums as found in "hot" contests.

In addition, there was little evidence from voter's standpoints regarding the implementation of voluntary codes of conduct. Only 32 percent of voters saw much evidence of conduct codes in their local congressional districts, and just 34 percent of voters indicated that candidates in their districts had taken a pledge to avoid negative campaigning. If the public sees scant evidence of reform, that perception is important for the political system. Reforms that are implemented, but are not visible, do little to improve public confidence in the campaign process.

Furthermore, for reform to be successful, voters must see a link between reform activities and improvements in the tone and substance of campaign communications. If individuals perceive more substantive candidate discussions taking place during debates or issue forums, not only would that make them feel better about those particular reforms, it possibly could also improve their assessments of the overall political process.

In examining the visibility of this reform, though, our surveys found that awareness was modest. When asked if they had heard of reform activities involving code of conduct pledges, only 17 percent of registered voters revealed some awareness and 80 percent were unaware. This suggests limited awareness of the reform and therefore a weak ability to affect the campaign process in the manner desired by reform organizations.[11]

The lack of voter familiarity with the reform is not surprising. Consistent with past electoral cycles, voters did not report a high level of knowledge of or engagement in the election. Forty-nine percent said they knew the name of the winning candidate in their local U.S. House race, while 37 percent did not and another 11 percent were not able to accurately name the winning candidate in their congressional district.

Only 29 percent of the voters we interviewed indicated that they had closely followed the election for U.S. House of Representatives in their district by reading newspaper accounts or by using other media to follow the campaign regularly. Thirty percent said they followed the race fairly closely, 23 percent said they watched it somewhat closely, 11 percent indicated they did not follow the campaign very closely, and 5 percent stated they did not follow the campaign at all.

When asked how informed they felt about various aspects of congressional campaigns, 55 percent of voters said they felt very or fairly informed of the candidates' backgrounds and qualifications, and 56 percent agreed concerning the candidate's records and issue positions. Similarly, 56 percent felt informed about national policy issues and 54 percent said they were informed about local policy issues.

This lack of knowledge on the part of ordinary citizens complicates the task of political reformers. It takes highly visible reform activities to draw citizen attention because many people do not pay close attention to the political process. Complex changes or reforms that are not easily understood have little chance of being noticed by the general electorate. With such a lack of overall visibility, they have even less chance of producing significant changes in campaign conduct. Since relatively few congressional campaigns are hotly contested – about 10 percent by most measures – it is not surprising that citizens paid little attention. As a consequence, it is not surprising that few saw the effects of any efforts at campaign reform.

The final group of perceptions we examined concerned views about the campaign. To ascertain if progress had been made toward this goal, we wanted to find out how citizens saw the midterm race in particular. By studying impressions about the campaign, we hoped to see whether voters believed that campaign reform had any relationship to those shifts.

In general, voters are skeptical of the ability of reforms to improve electoral discourse. For example, 39 percent of voters believed that a voluntary campaign code would be very or fairly effective at improving discourse, 30 percent argued it would be just somewhat effective, and 28 percent thought it would not be very effective. Of those voters who said a local congressional candidate had taken a campaign conduct pledge, 19 percent believed the candidate had done very well in living up to the pledge, 28 percent said fairly well, 22 percent felt it was lived up to somewhat well, and 26 percent felt it was not done very well.

Similar to the consultants, we asked voters three questions about the tone and specificity of campaign discourse: (1) Overall, voters are not happy with the style or substance of the midterm campaign. Compared to past elections, do you think that this year's election campaign was generally more positive, about the same, or more negative? (2) Compared to past elections, would you say that there was more discussion about policy issues in this campaign or less discussion about policy issues?

Table 2-3. Voter Feelings About
the Campaign

Tone of campaign	
negative	36
positive	17
Level of discussion	
less policy discussion	49
more policy discussion	27
Value of ads to voters	
ads helpful	20
ads hurtful	62

Values represent percentages.
Source: National Voter Survey, November 2002.

And (3) do you feel the campaign ads that ran in your district were generally helpful and added to your ability to understand the positions and qualifications of the two candidates and helped the election process, or do you feel that the ads were not helpful and were just aimed at providing negative information about the opponent and hurt the election process?

As shown in Table 2-3, 36 percent described the election as generally more negative than past elections, 17 percent believed it was more positive, and 43 percent indicated they thought the tone was about the same as in past years. When asked to compare the level of issue discussion with previous years, voters were more likely than consultants to see definitive changes in the level of discussion of policy issues. Twenty-seven percent of voters said they thought there had been more issue discussion (double the 11 percent of consultants who agreed), 49 percent believed there had been less discussion (more than the 32 percent of consultants who felt that way), and 16 percent thought it was a similar level to that in past years.

Citizens were much less positive than consultants about campaign ads run during the midterm elections. When asked if commercials broadcast in their district were generally helpful and added to their ability to understand the positions and qualifications of the candidates or were not helpful and merely attempted to provide negative information about the opponent, 62 percent described ads as hurting the election process, while 20 percent thought they were helpful. These reactions are nearly the opposite of the view taken by our national sample of consultants. Unsurprisingly, given their role in formulating campaign ads, campaign professionals were more likely than voters to think that such advertisements were helpful.

Judging from these comparisons, it is obvious that voters and consultants took away different impressions from the campaign air war. Whereas consultants believed the ads were more helpful, a clear majority of citizens thought ads hurt the process. Just as those "inside the Beltway" think that congressional campaigns dominate Americans' lives, when few in fact pay much attention at all, so too do those inside a campaign view the effect of their efforts as more effective than those at whom their efforts are aimed.

Despite citizen discontent with ad tone, though, twice as many voters indicated they were satisfied as unsatisfied with the election. Fifty-two percent of voters said they were pleased and satisfied with the outcome of the U.S. House race in their district, whereas 22 percent were displeased and dissatisfied, and 22 percent reported no strong feeling either way. There are no historical numbers on election satisfaction so it is not clear how to interpret these results.

One way to understand this result is that the respondents were pleased with who was elected, not with the process itself. However, we would expect more than half to be satisfied in this sense, because approximately that number voted for the winner. Another interpretation emphasizes the argument that in a democracy, we should expect more than 52 percent to express satisfaction with the process. Ideally, a high level of voter satisfaction should be the reformers' goal. From our standpoint, more than half of voters should feel satisfied with the overall election.

CONCLUSION

To conclude, campaign reform did not meet many of the tenets of an effectiveness test. While direct and straightforward reforms, such as debates and issue forums, achieved high visibility and awareness (especially among campaign professionals), harder-to-grasp changes, such as pledges to avoid negativity and pledges to obey conduct codes, were not visible to consultants or voters. Neither consultants nor voters were very optimistic about the prospects of these reforms for improving the style and substance of campaigning. Many were skeptical of conduct codes and did not trust the media to act as effective overseers of campaign discourse. Some thought conduct codes were inherently ineffective, while others believed they were too easy to evade.

Professional associations are limited as agents of effective self-regulation because most consultants do not belong to the AAPC or do not view this organization's current role or role to which it should aspire as an aggressive overseer of consulting behavior. The fact that few barriers block entry into the consulting profession makes it difficult for the AAPC to act as a strong regulator of personal conduct. We know of no evidence that at any point soon the AAPC will be powerful enough to serve as an effective sanctioning agent for the entire profession.

Given these weaknesses, it is not surprising that voters and consultants were not very positive about the tone and substance of the campaign. Many thought the campaign was negative and not very substantive in nature. Citizens were upset with the tone of campaign advertisements. They did not feel that the commercials were very helpful in understanding the campaign or highlighting substantive differences among the candidates. Consultants were more positive about the ads, but ordinary folks did not share this assessment.

Our conversations with consultants suggested that if campaign reform is to work, changes must be picked up by the media and publicized to the general public. Skeptics argued that only reforms that stand any chance of working are those that affect campaign dialogue and campaign strategies. They noted that the most effective outside groups are those that take partisan sides, not nonprofit and nonpartisan groups that attempt to stand above the political fray. In their eyes, reform ultimately is a political process and requires a keen understanding of politics. Reforms cannot take "politics" out of the political process and hope to be effective in improving the conduct of politicians.

THREE

Impact on Campaign Conduct

C ritics have leveled a variety of complaints at professional campaign-ers, from suggesting they use shrill and nonsubstantive rhetoric and have financial conflicts of interest to arguing that they rely on unfair, misleading, or deceptive electoral strategies. With the centrality of their function in democratic elections, it is crucial to understand the role consultants play during the electoral cycle and whether the presence of particular reforms is associated with improvements in the campaign.

Using data from our consultant survey, we argue that the relationship between particular reforms and various indicators of campaign conduct is not strong. Organizing debates or issue forums, having candidates who attend professional training schools, or getting campaigners to sign conduct codes is associated with some positive features of campaign conduct, but the relationship is not very consistent. No single reform is consistently linked to various measures of improved campaign conduct.

The reason for this lack of strong relationship is that most reform proposals do not fully appreciate the incentives facing many profes-sional campaigners. Rather than addressing the political and financial incentives that motivate these individuals, efforts to change campaign conduct play to a sense of civic responsibility or collective well-being for society as a whole. As a consequence of not understanding the incentives consultants have for campaign conduct, these reform proposals do not achieve their desired impact. These ideas simply are out of sync with the factors that govern the thinking and behavior of campaign elites.

THE PROFESSIONALIZATION OF CAMPAIGNS

American campaigns are very professional in how they approach the twin tasks of political communication and voter mobilization. As electoral contests have come to depend on media campaigns and large amounts of money in order to elicit citizen support, campaign professionals have taken a central role.[1] Most candidates for major offices in the United States, such as those for president, U.S. senator, U.S. representative, and governor, hire consultants who poll the public, design advertisements, raise money, and plot general strategy.[2]

Ever since John Kennedy employed Lou Harris to undertake surveys for him during the 1960 presidential campaign, candidates have spent hundreds of thousands of dollars each year, attempting to gauge public sentiment.[3] Pollsters measure what voters think and how candidates should communicate with them. What are the top issues in citizens' minds and what stances would bring the greatest number of votes to the candidate?

Media consultants advise candidates on advertising strategies. In presidential campaigns, roughly 60 percent of the overall budget is devoted to television ads, while in congressional races, ad expenditures comprise around 40 percent of the campaign budget.[4] Media advisors work in conjunction with pollsters and strategists to devise effective communications strategies for their candidates. Depending on which voter blocs are most important, these specialists produce spots that play to the hopes, fears, and concerns of the target audience.

One of the unintended results of campaign finance reform is the emergence of direct mail as a major part of political campaigns. The McCain–Feingold campaign finance bill targeted "sham" issue ads for major restrictions. Based on the bill's provisions, organizations that run advertisements featuring the name and likeness of a candidate less than 30 days before a primary or 60 days before a general election must disclose the names of contributors to their group (although federal judges later struck down some of these restrictions).

However, since the bill paid little attention to direct mail, phone banks, and Internet campaigning, these tactics have become beneficiaries of the drive to curtail issue advocacy. According to GOP direct mail consultant Dan Hazelwood, "It's also another symbol of how moronic the campaign finance reform bill was. All it did was push down on whatever irritated McCain and Feingold at the moment." Continuing, he added, "It will drive a lot of folks to expand their direct-mail campaigns, without a doubt, and there will be even less of a way to track who did it."[5]

This impression was confirmed in a survey of political consultants, conducted by American University. When asked how they thought the new campaign law would affect the consulting industry, survey supervisor James Thurber said, "Media people are worried . . . and direct-mail people like what they're seeing." About one-third of the consultants believe the legislation will strengthen the role of state parties and one-third believe it will hurt the role of national party organizations.[6]

Regardless of which medium is most advantaged, fund-raisers will undoubtedly become among the most important beneficiaries in this era of high-tech campaigning. Polling, television ads, and direct mail are expensive and candidates must raise enormous sums of money in order to hire individuals who specialize in these areas. Fund-raisers who know which individuals will give (and what kinds of causes those people support) are indispensable in any kind of major campaign in the United States.

CONSULTANTS, CANDIDATES, AND CAMPAIGN CONDUCT

In looking at the role that consultants and candidates play in campaign conduct, political observers have worried about a range of problems. Some consultants have been accused of engaging in unethical or misleading behavior. Larry Sabato and Glenn Simpson, for example, discussed how one consultant in a Minnesota congressional race engaged in unethical phone calls. Hoping to plant the rumor that a female candidate was a lesbian, his firm placed hundreds of calls asking unsuspecting voters whether their support would be affected if they thought the candidate were a lesbian.[7]

Other candidates and consultants have used emotional appeals designed to convey negative impressions of the opponent. In 1988, Republican presidential candidate George H. W. Bush used the story of Willie Horton, a convicted felon who raped a woman while out on furlough from a Massachusetts prison, to convince voters that his opponent, Michael Dukakis, the governor of Massachusetts, was soft on crime.[8] And in 1964, a Lyndon Johnson ad known as "Daisy" sparked an outcry with its controversial message about the threat of nuclear war if Republican Barry Goldwater were elected.

A recent congressional primary in Chicago degenerated into what one candidate complained was ethnic name-calling. A Polish-American supporter of Democrat Nancy Kaszak criticized opponent Rahm Emanuel, who is Jewish, for being a "millionaire carpetbagger" and said that a Polish-American newspaper that sold advertising space to Emanuel was guilty of "betray[ing] Polonia." Emanuel complained that the comments "weren't criticisms of Rahm Emanuel as an individual. Those statements, the meaning behind those statements, were criticisms of me as a Jewish American."[9]

The nonsubstantive nature of these appeals creates difficulties in elections, which require voters to choose between competing candidates. If citizens need help in evaluating opponents, they often do not get much assistance from the candidates themselves. Rather than helping people to understand differences and judge the candidates accordingly, some campaign rhetoric obfuscates much more than it clarifies.

Research by James Thurber of American University and his associates indicates that "one-half of the consultants surveyed said that unethical practices occur either 'very often' or 'sometimes' in campaigns." Furthermore, 38 percent of those consultants surveyed say that the use of scare tactics in elections is acceptable, 48 percent believe it is questionable, and only 13 percent think it is clearly unethical. However, despite these findings, Thurber argues that much of the unfavorable portrait that exists for campaign consultants is unfair. According to him, his data "do not support the negative view of their profession portrayed in the popular media."[10]

Others, though, worry that consultants are responsible for driving campaigns toward greater negativity, increased use of unfair tactics, and a decline in the civility of political discourse. If unethical practices on the scale reported by the American University survey project are taking place in contemporary campaigns, it is a serious problem for the entire political system.

THE LINK BETWEEN CAMPAIGN REFORM AND IMPROVED CAMPAIGNS

To analyze the connection between reform and campaign conduct, we compare races where there were reports of debates, issues forums, voluntary codes of conduct, and staff training with various measures of campaign discourse and conduct. Among other things, we look at views about campaign tone, issue discussion, and voter turnout to see if there are any positive relationships with different reform measures.

Our goal is to see whether there is any association between districts with and without debates, for example, and impressions about the style and substance of campaigning in those areas. If districts having debates also tend to exhibit higher levels of policy discussion and more positive campaigns, it provides some evidence of an association between specific reforms and improved campaign conduct. This would strengthen the arguments of optimist reformers that their initiatives are successful.

Of course, correlations do not prove causality. We cannot definitively argue that specific reforms caused the desirable outcome. However, an association between the two would lend credibility to the arguments of advocates that their efforts were paying off in more effective performance. Conversely, finding no tie or a negative association between the presence or absence of reform and improved campaign conduct would allow us to infer that the efforts of the reform community were not bearing fruit. The absence of a strong and consistent association would suggest that reform implementation in congressional districts was not linked to better campaigns.

To test these connections, we asked consultants in the most competitive House and Senate races to describe various features of their local campaign. Among other aspects, we quizzed them on whether the tone of their local congressional campaign had been positive or negative, whether the level of policy discussion was higher or lower than in previous years, whether turnout had gone up, and whether ads were helpful to voters.

We realize these measures of campaign quality are perceptual in nature, based on the views of partisan observers (i.e., campaign consultants). But since our sample included a representative mix of Republicans and Democrats as well as winning and losing consultants, we argue that these views provide relevant indicators of what happened in those races. In the next chapter, we rely on the independent assessments of unaligned academic observers in competitive districts to provide more objective measures of campaign discourse and tone.

In examining the views of campaign consultants, we found that the occurrence of formal debates between congressional candidates was seen as having a positive association with consultants' views about the lack of negativity of the overall campaign. For example, in Table 3-1, districts with formal debates showed less negativity than those where debates did not occur. In the latter case, 50 percent of those surveyed stated that the overall tone of the election was more negative than previous elections, compared to 39 percent who felt that way in races where debates did happen (an 11 percentage point difference).

However, this pattern in favor of reform did not hold up when consultants were asked about the tone of their own congressional campaign. Whereas 44 percent of those whose candidates did not participate in a

Table 3-1. Consultant Impressions of Campaign by Existence of Formal Debates Between Candidates

	Formal Debates	No Formal Debates
Overall tone more negative	39 (70)	50 (9)
Tone in own campaign negative	61 (109)	44 (8)
Less issue discussion	30 (53)	50 (9)
Campaign ads helped voters	52 (93)	44 (8)
Voter turnout increased	54 (96)	22 (4)

Values represent percentages; *N* for number of responses in that category is in parentheses.
Source: Campaign Consultant Survey, November 2002.

debate argued that the campaign was negative, 61 percent of those whose candidates did participate in debates thought the tone was negative. This perception is contrary to the expectations of the reform model. Rather than being associated with an improvement of tone, as was true for the campaign as a whole, consultants did not feel there was a less negative campaign in their local race when a debate was present.

Debate participation does appear to improve the level of policy discussion in the campaign. For instance, while only one-in-three consultants whose candidates participated in formal debates argued that there was less issue discussion in their race, half of those whose candidates did not participate in debates posited that the discussion of issues had dropped. Similarly, consultants whose candidates had participated in debates were 8 percent more likely than those who had not to argue that the campaign ads which had run in the race had helped voters to better understand candidate qualifications and issue positions. They were also more than twice as likely (54 to 22 percent) to say that voter turnout had increased in their race. This shows that debates are associated with improved discourse in some situations.

Table 3-2 demonstrates that the existence of issue forums in which both major candidates appeared also seemed to have a positive impact on campaign conduct. For example, consultants whose candidates had appeared in issue forums were 14 percent less likely to state that the overall tone of the electoral cycle was more negative than in previous elections. Again, however, results regarding the particular race on which consultants worked went against the general grain. While 61 percent of consultants whose candidates had participated argued that their particular race was more negative than in previous cycles, only 52 percent of those whose clients had not participated in such forums agreed.

Table 3-2. Consultant Impressions of Campaign by Existence of Issue Forums

	Issue Forums	No Issue Forums
Overall tone more negative	38 (61)	52 (15)
Tone in own campaign negative	61 (98)	52 (15)
Less issue discussion	30 (48)	41 (12)
Voter turnout increased	55 (89)	31 (9)
Campaign ads helped voters	52 (83)	48 (14)
Pledge not improve campaign behavior	47 (76)	48 (14)

Values represent percentages; *N* for subcategory is in parentheses.
Source: Campaign Consultant Survey, November 2002.

Table 3-3. Consultant Impressions of Campaign by Existence of Code of Conduct

	Code of Conduct Pledge	No Pledge
Overall tone more negative	36 (18)	41 (56)
Tone in own campaign negative	56 (28)	63 (86)
Less issue discussion	26 (13)	33 (45)
Campaign ads helped voters	58 (29)	49 (67)
Aware of IGE reform efforts	44 (22)	29 (40)
Pledge not improve campaign behavior	42 (21)	51 (70)
Voter turnout increased	46 (23)	54 (74)

Values represent percentages; *N* for subcategory is in parentheses.
Source: Campaign Consultant Survey, November 2002.

Despite this result, the presence of issue forums was associated with a generally positive effect on the consultants' views of the campaigns in which they worked. While only three-in-ten of those whose clients participated in issue forums judged that the cycle had less issue discussion than previous cycles, over four-in-ten of those whose candidates had not participated agreed.

Although they resulted in smaller disparities, whether one or both candidates took a code of conduct campaign pledge also seemed to be associated with positive consultant assessments of campaign conduct. For example, as seen in Table 3-3, consultants whose candidates took a code of conduct pledge were 5 percent less likely to describe the overall tone of the elections as more negative than previous cycles. They also were 7 percent less likely to describe the race on which they worked as more negative than previous campaigns. Similarly, only 26 percent of consultants who worked on campaigns where at least one candidate took the pledge described their race as having less issue discussion than previous campaigns, while one-in-three consultants working on races where candidates did not take a pledge of conduct agreed. The latter group was less likely (49–58 percent) than consultants working on races where at least one candidate had taken a pledge to argue that the campaign ads which ran in the race helped inform voters about the candidates' qualifications and issue positions.

Consultants who worked in races where at least one candidate took a code of conduct pledge were more likely (44 to 29 percent) than those working races where neither candidate did so to be aware of IGE reform efforts or those of other related organizations. But they were less likely (42 percent) than their counterparts to argue that such a pledge had no effect on improving campaign behavior. Indeed, 51 percent of consultants in races where candidates had not taken a conduct pledge argued that such pledges do not improve campaign behavior.

It seems, then, that those consultants who worked on a race where at least one candidate took a code of conduct pledge were more likely to view it as having a positive impact on campaigning. Nonetheless, consultants working on races where no candidate took the pledge were 8 percent more likely to argue that voter turnout increased in their race over previous cycles. This finding gives credence to the belief that negative discourse activates a campaign's core voters, driving *up* turnout, not depressing it as argued by some academics.[11] It could also be the result of level of competition in the two sets of races.

Similar to the code of conduct pledge, the perceptual differences between consultants who worked on races where a candidate took a pledge to avoid negative campaigning and those who did not were minor, as revealed in Table 3-4. The biggest differences between these consultants regarded whether or not they believed the overall tone of the electoral cycle was negative and whether or not they felt that the campaign ads which ran in their race helped voters. While 35 percent of consultants working on races where at least one candidate took the pledge to avoid negative campaigning argued that the overall tone was more negative, 44 percent of those working on campaigns in which no candidate took such a pledge held that view.

In the same vein, those working on campaigns where the pledge was taken by at least one candidate were 13 percent more likely than consultants working in races where no pledge was taken to believe that the ads run in the race helped voters to better understand the candidates' qualifications and issue stances. Less dramatically, consultants working

Table 3-4. Consultant Impressions of Campaign by Existence of Pledge
to Avoid Negative Campaigning

	Pledge to Avoid Negative Campaigning	No-Negative-Campaign Pledge
Overall tone more negative	35 (20)	44 (58)
Campaign ads helped voters	60 (35)	47 (63)
Pledge not improve campaign behavior	45 (26)	50 (67)
Tone in own campaign negative	59 (34)	61 (81)
Voter turnout increased	53 (31)	51 (68)
Less issue discussion	29 (17)	33 (44)

Values represent percentages; N for subcategory is in parentheses.
Source: Campaign Consultant Survey, November 2002.

on races where a pledge was taken were slightly less likely (45–50 percent) than their brethren to argue that pledges to run positive campaigns have no effect on improving campaign behavior.

Consultants who did or did not work on campaigns in which a candidate agreed to take a pledge to avoid negative campaigning expressed similar impressions of campaign conduct. For instance, roughly six-in-ten of each category of consultants argued that the tone in their own campaign was more negative than in past cycles. Roughly half of each type of consultants argued that voter turnout had increased in their race over previous midterm election cycles. And, last, about one-in-three of each consultant category believed that there was less issue discussion than in previous cycles.

These results demonstrate that there is no association between taking a no-negative-campaigning pledge and these measures of campaign conduct. Having a pledge produced no improvement in campaign tone, voter turnout, or level of issue discussion. Not only do these findings run contrary to the prediction of a reform model, they cast doubt on the view that negativity is a uniformly unfavorable aspect of contemporary campaigns.

Drawing contrasts between the candidates, which some observers interpret as negative campaigning, can provide policy information to voters. It also can crystallize differences between candidates and provide a motivation for some citizens to cast ballots on election day.

To summarize, our bivariate results demonstrate that there are some positive associations between campaign reform and campaign conduct, but the relationships are not uniformly present nor very robust in nature. Percentage differences tend to be rather small between districts where certain reforms were present or absent. Sometimes, the results run in the opposite direction to that predicted by a successful reform model. This preliminary assessment does not generate high confidence in the ability of proposed reforms to improve contemporary elections in the United States.

A MULTIVARIATE ASSESSMENT OF CAMPAIGN REFORM AND CONDUCT

Bivariate cross-tabulations are helpful in pinpointing the relationship between particular reforms and campaign conduct, but they cannot prove that such associations exist. There always is the possibility that other factors affect the relationships under consideration. Since many factors may affect campaign tone, issue discussion, and voter turnout, it is important to undertake multivariate assessments of campaign conduct.

Using our campaign consultant survey, we looked at the association between campaign conduct and each of five reform proposals (having formal debates, holding issue forums, pledges by candidates to abide by a specific code of campaign conduct, pledges to avoid negative campaigning, and staff or candidate attendance at a campaign training school). We examined the consequences of each proposal individually because few districts had all the changes present simultaneously. At best, most areas had one, two, or three reforms in their local campaigns.[12]

In addition to investigating the effect of each individual proposal, we created an overall campaign reform index consisting of the sum of the five campaign reforms. This scale measured whether 0, 1, 2, 3, 4, or 5 of these reform initiatives took place in the local congressional district. This helped us to study the cumulative effect of reform and determine whether districts in which many reforms were implemented had better campaigns than areas where fewer were.

In each regression, we controlled for several factors shown to be relevant for campaign conduct: the consultant's party, the consultant's age, whether the consultant was on the winning side of the congressional race, whether the incumbent worked for an incumbent seeking reelection, and the region of the country where the election campaign took place. These are factors that have been demonstrated in the electoral behavior area to be important predictors of how campaigners think and act.[13]

Eighteen separate regressions were undertaken for the five initiatives, as well as the overall reform index, on three different dependent variables: campaign tone (measured by whether the consultant thought that the campaign was generally more positive, had about the same tone, or was generally more negative than recent election cycles), campaign issue discussion (measured by whether the consultant thought there was more discussion of policy issues in the campaign, about the same amount of discussion, or less issue discussion than past election cycles), and voter turnout (measured by whether the consultant believed that voter turnout in the race in which they were involved went down, stayed the same, or went up compared to the last midterm election).

For most of the 18 models tested, there were no significant linkages between the reform activities and measures of campaign conduct. For example, having debates or issue forums in the race was not associated with a more positive campaign tone or more issue discussion. The same thing happened in regard to pledges to avoid negative campaigning. There were no significant associations between these kinds of pledges and improvements in campaign tone, issue discussion, or voter turnout. There was no tie at the multivariate level between campaign staff or the candidate attending a campaign training school and improving campaign tone or raising voter turnout.

Finding null relationships confirms the skeptics' view of no-negative pledges reported by consultants in the preceding chapter. In our in-depth interviews and focus groups, political consultants did not have a high opinion or think they would improve campaign conduct. Our statistical analysis based on this survey dovetails with the conclusions of the other methodologies.

However, as shown in Table 3-5, there was a significant link on 5 of the 18 connections. For example, there was a significant association between having debates and higher voter turnout. Districts in which consultants said there were formal debates in which both major congressional candidates participated tended to have higher voter turnout, even after controlling for the other factors in the model.

A similar result was found in regard to issue forums. District races in which issue forums took place at which both major candidates appeared were associated with consultants believing that voter turnout went up. This suggests that these kinds of forums produce a positive result in terms of the important goal of voter engagement. Citizens pay attention to debates and forums and reporters cover them. This helps to engage the public in civic life and draw people to the ballot box.

There was a significant association between candidates' pledges to abide by a specific code of conduct in running their campaigns and a more positive campaign tone. Races where such pledges were made were

Table 3-5. Regression Results for Campaign Reform on Consultant Views About Campaign Tone, Issue Discussion, and Voter Turnout

	Tone	Tone	Issue Discussion	Turnout	Turnout
Formal debates	—	—	—	.50 (.22)*	—
Issue forums	—	—	—	—	.54 (.18)**
Code of conduct	−.29 (.10)**	—	—	—	—
Campaign training	—	—	.23 (.10)*	—	—
Summary campaign reform index	—	−.10 (.04)*	—	—	—
Consultant's party identification	−.18 (.05)***	−.19 (.05)***	−.21 (.05)***	−.06 (.07)	−.07 (.07)
Consultant age	−.09 (.04)*	−.09 (.05)	−.04 (.04)	.03 (.06)	.02 (.06)
Won race	−.11 (.10)	−.12 (.11)	−.04 (.10)	−.27 (.14)*	−.25 (.13)
Worked for incumbent	−.22 (.12)	−.16 (.14)	−.05 (.13)	.14 (.17)	.20 (.17)
Race was in South/ non-South	−.07 (.10)	−.03 (.11)	−.14 (.10)	.16 (.14)	.17 (.14)
Constant	3.46 (.27)***	3.89 (.43)***	2.47 (.27)***	1.81 (.52)***	1.77 (.44)***
Adjusted R^2	.12	.10	.14	.04	.07
F statistic	5.03***	3.80***	5.27***	2.18*	3.11**
N	181	156	162	162	159

*$p < .05$; **$p < .01$; ***$p < .001$.
Note: The numbers are unstandardized regression coefficients, with standard errors in parentheses. The number of asterisks indicates the statistical significance of the coefficient.

Source: Campaign Consultant Survey, November 2002.

associated with districts where the consultants believed that there was a more positive tone to the campaign discussions.

There was a significant relationship between campaign training schools and issue discussion, but in a direction contrary to that anticipated by reformers. Consultants who reported having campaign staff who attended training schools said there was less issue discussion in their campaign.

The paucity of positive consequences related to training casts doubt on those seeking a long-term reform payoff from improved professionalization of the consulting industry. The hope was that by providing formal training, consultants would learn about ethical practices and use this instruction to improve campaign conduct. But there is little evidence from the consultant survey that these aspirations are being met or that this reform model is very effective.

After looking at the impact of each individual reform item, we developed an overall campaign reform index consisting of a scale measuring how many of the five reforms were present in the race where the consultant worked. We regressed this on our three indicators of quality campaigns (tone, issue discussion, and voter turnout), controlling for factors also thought to be important in electoral behavior.

In this analysis, we found that there was a significant tie with having a more positive tone, but no association with issue discussion or voter turnout. With all the reform items taken together, there was no improvement in the level of substantive discussion or in how engaged and active citizens became in the election. This suggests the limited ability of reform efforts to produce desired changes in campaign conduct during House and Senate elections.

CONCLUSION

To summarize, our results demonstrate that perceptions about sponsoring debates or issue forums, having candidates who attend professional training schools, or getting campaigners to sign conduct codes have some benefits for campaign conduct, as hypothesized by campaign reform optimists. In our multivariate results with statistical controls, reforms such as debates and issue forums were associated with perceptions about increased turnout; and candidate conduct codes were linked to impressions of a more positive campaign tone. These results are in line with electoral theories, suggesting that reform improves campaign conduct and enhances views about the tone of and participation in the electoral process.

However, the reform relationship with campaign conduct is neither consistently positive nor uniformly strong. On the less favorable side, pledges to avoid negativity had no significant associations with campaign quality, and attendance at professional campaign schools actually was associated with decreases in the level of policy discussion. The latter conclusion, of course, runs completely contrary to the hopes of reformers. Reformers hoped that by professionalizing the industry, these training schools would improve campaign conduct and add to the substance of political discussions. But there was little evidence that those hopes were realized.

Speaking more generally, these findings suggest that reform type matters and that various reforms have different consequences. Straightforward reforms such as debates and forums are the simplest for voters to grasp. Voters understand them, they are easy to cover on the part of the media, and they increase campaign interest and voter participation.

Other reforms such as no-negativity pledges are more complex to understand and are not very visible. These qualities make it far more difficult to implement effectively. Candidates can manipulate these pledges by going negative while also accusing opponents of starting the negativity and a lack of civility. Or they can stay positive, while surrogates walk the low road of negativity. Neither result helps voters understand electoral choices or does much to improve accountability and representation in the political system.

With all the reforms, it is clear that for advocates to be most effective, proposals must be tied to the real world in which consultants live. The problem with some reforms is that they do not fully appreciate the incentives facing professional campaigners. Rather than addressing the motivations of these individuals, advocates seek to appeal to the civic responsibility of these individuals. These rationales tend not to be very effective because professional campaigners do not take "good government" appeals very seriously.

As a consequence, some reform proposals do not achieve their desired impact. If they do not address motivations that are clearly present and important to campaigners, political professionals will ignore the suggestion. Reforms that are visible to reporters and citizens matter because of the possibility of either reward or punishment flowing from these actions. The most effective reforms are those that are salient to the forces that have consequences for political professionals.

FOUR

Impact on Campaign Discourse

In recent years, there has been considerable concern about the tone, style, and content of political campaigns. In many races, by the time of voting, "ad fatigue" grips the voters. The arrival of Election Day is not seen as a time to celebrate democracy but rather as a period to be thankful that campaign ads no longer litter the airways. There is a more fundamental sense in which Election Day is not seen as the fruition of the nation's democratic electoral process. As Figure 4-1 reveals, turnout in presidential elections has hovered around 50 percent for the last eight elections; turnout in congressional elections, especially those held in nonpresidential years has been considerably lower.[1]

Political reformers feel that citizen discontent is the result, in part at least, of the content of electoral campaigns. To be sure, voters are bombarded with campaign messages of all types, with television and radio ads, with direct mail, with telephone messages, with literature on the doorstep, with speeches, Web sites, and more. These messages and the campaigns are covered on television and in the newspapers. Candidates debate each other in front of a variety of audiences, most often in person but on important occasions before media audiences. But the relevant question is whether the delivered messages are those the voters need to receive.[2]

Theories of democracy differ in terms of criteria for campaign effectiveness, but virtually all democratic theorists would agree that for representative democracy to function effectively, a minimal standard is that the voters must be given a choice and that they must understand that choice. That is, the substance of campaign discourse that reaches the voters must make clear to those voters what distinguishes one candidate from another. Those distinctions might be based on experience, on past record, on proven ability, on positions on the issues of the day, on the

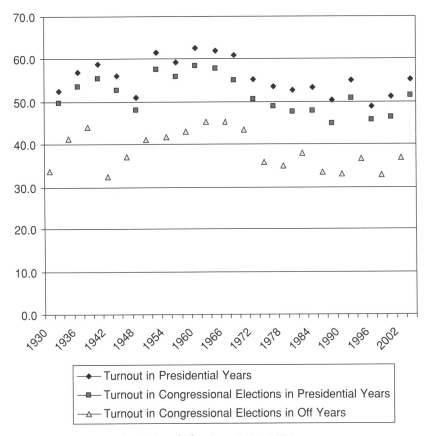

Figure 4-1. Turnout in National Elections, 1930–2004.

ability to accomplish goals, or on a number of other relevant factors, but those distinctions must relate to voters' perceptions of what is important in the person who should represent them.

In addition, there is ample evidence that voters care about the type of person who represents them. At the most basic level, citizens want to be proud of their representatives, of the kinds of people they are. They also want a sense that the representative understands people like them. In Richard Fenno's term, citizens care about a representatives "home style."[3] They want to be able to relate to their representative in a positive way.

Dissatisfaction with recent campaigns stems from failure to meet either of these voter needs. Campaign messages tend to be extremely short, full of imagery, and lacking in relevant content. What content exists typically is negative – giving the voters a reason not to vote for an opponent, rather than a positive reason to support the candidate sponsoring the ad or mailing the piece of literature. Campaigns are run in this way because they have proven to be effective in terms of winning. As one consultant put it to us, "We are paid to win, not to make the public feel good. We run negative campaigns because negative campaigns help our candidates win. That's our job."

The media covering campaigns often report on the campaign strategy and tactics, on who is winning and who is losing, on who is "going negative" and who is not. The media are seen as contributing little to encouraging substantive campaigns. Rarely do the media sort out differences on issues that the campaigns themselves seek to obscure.[4] True debates among candidates are rare. More often debates seem to be opportunities for candidates to present pre-scripted answers to predictable questions or to attack their opponents on seeming vulnerabilities. Candidates follow these strategies because they have proven to be successful.

But with that electoral success comes a real loss for the polity. Citizens become cynical. They choose not to vote rather than to support either of the candidates who have been beating up on each other. They lose respect for officeholders, because a barrage of negative publicity tends to lead one to believe the messages that are delivered – and one of those candidates running eventually wins. Good people decide not to run for office. Who would want to be involved in a process like this one?[5] Who would want to expose their families to such treatment?

Two changes are thus needed to improve the quality of campaign discourse. First, campaigns need to become less negative and citizens need to be given a reason to vote *for* a candidate rather than a reason to vote *against* a candidate. Second, the substantive message needs to be enhanced. Citizens want to know where candidates stand on the issues (at least in general terms), what qualifications they would bring to the office, how they would represent the district – each of these in concrete terms, not in meaningless platitudes.

COMMUNICATING THE CAMPAIGN'S MESSAGE

In recent years, particularly in races lower down the ballot, few campaigns have seen intense competition. While the presidency as the top prize is always intensely fought over and while most governorships and seats in the U.S. Senate draw competitive candidates, in recent years only about

10 percent of the elections for seats in the U.S. House of Representatives and even a lower percentage of seats in state legislatures are competed for intensely.

The detailed reasons for the lack of competition for less visible offices stem from redistricting that creates districts heavily favoring one party or another.[6] In addition, noncompetitiveness arises from advantages that incumbents have in seeking reelection, such as name identification, fund-raising, media coverage, and interest group support. Finally, many "down-ballot" contests are uncompetitive simply due to a lack of voter interest in the offices being contested.

In this study, we focus on those races that are competitive because it is in these that the most egregious examples of nonsubstantive, negative campaigns are likely to be seen.[7] Most Senate races are competitively fought (even if the end result is not close) because the stakes are so high. The election is for a 6-year term and control of the Senate hangs in the balance when a small number of seats shift.

Similarly, in the House of Representatives, most open seats are hotly contested. When incumbents run, they are difficult to beat; therefore, when an incumbent is not on the ballot, ambitious politicians see a chance to move up. Often both primaries and general elections are hotly contested in open seats. In election years following reapportionment and redistricting, those races in which one incumbent is pitted against another tend to be hotly contested – as each person's job is on the line. Finally, a relatively small number of incumbents face serious challengers; typically, these are incumbents who have faced some sort of scandal, who have cast highly visible and controversial votes, who are running in districts the partisan makeup of which favors the other party, or who have been seriously challenged in the immediate past. While reformers should be concerned with all of these races, analysts also will note differences, because of the size of the constituency (especially large states vs. congressional districts), because of the presence or absence of an incumbent (with a record to defend or attack), and because of previous relationships that candidates might have had with each other (especially in incumbent vs. incumbent races).

In competitive elections – in fact in all elections – candidates communicate with the citizenry in two ways. First, they attempt to control the message that gets across through a variety of paid media – television, radio, and print advertisements, direct mail, leaflets, telephonic messages, Web sites. The advantage of these kinds of messages for a campaign is that they control the content and, to some extent, the intended audience.[8] The disadvantage, of course, is that these media cost money, a resource often in scarce supply.

As a result, campaigns also expend a good deal of time and energy to receive free media – coverage in the newspapers and on television as the prime examples. Candidates also participate in debates, some before small audiences, some before large, some broadcast throughout a district or at least in part of it. Free media have obvious advantages as well. First, because the message does not come directly from the candidate, it is seen as more authoritative, less biased. Second, it often reaches a large audience. Third, of course, free media are free; they do not expend the scarce resource of money that then can be used to buy more paid media.

But free media have disadvantages as well. The most significant disadvantage is that the campaign cannot control the message that goes out. In an interview, for instance, the message the candidate conveys is dependent, in large part, on the question the interviewer poses. The tone of the interview is outside of the candidate's control. Which answers are edited in and which out are also determined by the broadcast media, not the candidate. The audience is outside of the campaign's control. Campaign consultants work hard to "control" the free media climate their candidates face, but that control is never more than partial. It is a rare campaign that praises the free media for their objectivity and comprehensiveness. More frequently one hears complaints that one candidate was not covered adequately or that the other candidate's obvious failings were not reported.

Campaign discourse as heard by the voters is a combination of the free media coverage provided by newspapers, television, and radio – including the coverage of any debates that are held – and the total of the paid media by all of the candidates. In this chapter, we will examine all aspects of the campaign messages conveyed in the competitive House and Senate races. We focus first on the paid media and then on the coverage of the campaigns by the free media. We look at the messages that were conveyed and ascertain the effect, if any, that various reform proposals had in refining these messages.

THE ADVERTISING DATA SETS

We gathered data on campaign discourse in 22 competitive House races and 5 Senate races during the electoral season. These data were gathered by independent academic analysts in each district or state, following a protocol that had been carefully tested.[9] Of the House races, 4 involved districts in which one incumbent was running against another (CT-5, IL-19, MS-3, and PA-17), 9 were seats in which incumbents faced serious challengers (CT-2, FL-22, KS-3, MD-8 [incumbent Connie Morella, R, lost], MN-2 [incumbent Bill Luther, D, lost], NC-8, TX-23, UT-2, and WA-2), and the rest were open seats (AZ-1 [new seat after reapportionment], CO-7 [new seat], IN-2, ME-2, NV-3 [new seat], NH-1, NM-2, OH-3, and OH-17).

Where appropriate, we have analyzed the campaigns run in each type of race separately. The five Senate races we studied (ME, NH, MN, NC, and TX) were chosen because early in the campaign year they all looked to be competitive. While it would make some sense to break these down along similar lines and while there are real differences among these states along a number of different dimensions, for example, size of population, number of media markets, we analyze these as a group because the total number (and therefore the number of observations of each of our variables) is so small.

Obviously, partisan differences occur during any campaign; our design was sensitive to these differences. Of the advertisements we observed, 52 percent were sponsored by Republican candidates or organizations favoring Republican candidates; 47 percent were sponsored by or paid for by Democratic candidates.[10] Over half of these ads were paid for by candidate organizations (52 percent); 32 percent were paid for by party committees; and the remaining 15 percent by independent organizations.

Our assumption was that if campaign reform efforts had any effect, that effect should be observable in competitive elections. Thus, we examined campaign discourse in each of these races closely. We looked first at all aspects of media generated by the campaigns themselves. We developed a protocol, followed in all of the races, to examine campaign ads, campaign literature, speeches, telephone calls, leaflets, and so on. Table 4-1 shows the frequencies with which we observed each type of campaign media.

Campaign Web sites have been transformed from a campaign frill to a necessity over the last decade. Web sites are used for various purposes. John McCain's campaign for the Republican presidential nomination in 2000 and Howard Dean's Democratic presidential bid in 2004 demonstrated the effectiveness of the Internet as a fund-raising tool;

Table 4-1. Types of Media Observed

	Frequency	Percent
Campaign literature	98	7.8
Direct mail	501	40.1
Radio advertisement	36	2.9
Television ad	574	46.0
Phone call	38	3.0
Campaign speech	2	0.2
Total	1,249	100.0

Source: Campaign Advertising Data Set, 2002.

congressional candidates could not ignore that lesson. Other campaigns have used the Web as a means of drawing and then coordinating volunteers. Many use the Web to display their advertisements, press releases, and other forms of campaign discourse.[11]

Based on these uses of the Internet, we developed a protocol to analyze content of candidate Web pages. We observed the Web pages periodically throughout the campaign. In all, we have 174 observations of Web pages, examining not only the content, but also the ease of access and of information retrieval. We examine each of these aspects of paid campaign discourse separately. In each case our objective is to see how easily and accurately citizens can evaluate candidates for office and whether the tone of the campaigns reflected positively or negatively on the candidates involved.

Campaign Advertising

We are concerned with the overall tone of the campaigns and with the content of campaign discourse. Much of the tone is set by paid media advertising; similarly much of what candidates communicate concerning their views of issues comes from various media presentations that originate from their organization or from organizations favoring their candidacies, like political parties or interest groups.

Table 4-2 presents an analysis of overall evaluation of the media examined. For each of the questions, we asked coders to rank the ad under examination on a 5-point scale, from low issue content to high issue content, from extremely biased to not biased, and from strongly negative to strongly positive.[12] How one interprets these data depends on the standard one uses. If one looks at issue content, only 32 percent of the ads were in the two highest categories, 40 percent in the two lowest. It

Table 4-2. Overall Evaluations of Content of Advertisements

	Issue Content (%)	Bias (%)	Tone (%)
1. Low/extreme bias/strongly negative	18	10	21
2.	22	16	10
3.	28	32	16
4.	23	27	15
5. High/no bias/strongly positive	9	15	38
N	1,238	1,202	1,244

Source: Campaign Advertising Data Set, 2002.

is difficult to see these data as not indicating a continuing problem of providing low issue information to citizens.

However, for the other two factors, more ads fell into the two positive categories than in the two negative. Still, over a quarter of the ads fell near the extreme bias end of the scale, over 30 percent near the strongly negative end of the scale. If the goal of recent campaign reform efforts has been to improve overall campaign discourse, having that many ads evaluated with these clearly negative characteristics does not give one much confidence that the tone of the campaigns improved over earlier years. We clearly do not have comparative data from previous campaigns, but nothing in these data provides cause for optimism.

Another frequent set of complaints holds that political campaigns are bringing down the public's view of politicians and government officials overall in order to enhance their own standing with the voters. Years ago, Richard Fenno characterized this phenomenon as "running for Congress by running against the Congress."[13] This kind of negativism was not as apparent in the election cycle we observed. Only 10 percent of the ads were coded in one of the two most negative characterizations of portrayal of government institutions, 14 percent of portrayals of government officials, and 15 percent of government policies.

These data can be broken down to provide a more detailed picture of the discourse under study. Table 4-3 shows party differences. In each cell we present those evaluating the piece of campaign communication as characterized in one of the top two categories. Party differences are readily apparent on issue content (higher content for Democrats), bias (more biased ads from Republicans), and negativity (more strongly negative ads from Republicans). Smaller differences appear in the other variables examined, but the direction of the differences remains constant, with Republican ads less positive and less informative than Democratic ads.

Table 4-3. Percentage of Campaign Communication Having Various Qualities, By Party

	Republican (%)	Democrat (%)
High issue content	25	40
Highly relevant character information	14	22
Biased issue presentation	35	15
Specific issue statements	9	13
Negative overall tone	35	26
Negative about government institutions	9	12
Negative about government officials	12	15
Negative about government policies	12	16

Maximum $N = 1,263$ observations.
Source: Campaign Advertising Data Set, 2002.

Table 4-4. Percentage of Campaign Communication Having Various Qualities, By Type of Sponsor

	Candidate	Noncandidate	Total N
High issue content	29 (638)	36 (566)	1,227
Highly relevant character information	21 (641)	15 (564)	1,228
Biased issue presentation	17 (615)	36 (557)	1,195
Specific issue statements	9 (639)	13 (562)	1,224
Negative overall tone	17 (641)	45 (569)	1,233
Negative about government institutions	10 (642)	10 (558)	1,223
Negative about government officials	13 (642)	15 (567)	1,228
Negative about government policies	14 (642)	15 (569)	1,234

Values represent percentages; N for subcategory is in parentheses.
Source: Campaign Advertising Data Set, 2002.

How can one explain this partisan difference? Tables 4-4 and 4-5 provide a partial explanation. In Table 4-4 we see that campaign communications not sponsored by candidate organizations themselves fall higher on the negative qualities than do those sponsored by the candidates themselves. In Table 4-5 we see that more of those communications came from Republican party organizations than from Democrats. Our interviews with industry leaders confirm these findings. Most consultants agree that much of the negativity in campaigning came in late in the campaigns and that much of it was not sponsored by the candidates themselves.

The consultants we interviewed had various explanations for these results. According to one:

Table 4-5. Noncandidate Sponsored
Advertisements, By Party

Republicans	59 (338)
Democrats	40 (229)
N	578

Values represent percentages; *N* for subcategory
is in parentheses.
Source: Campaign Advertising Data Set, 2002.

And we were, as a campaign team, deathly afraid as being perceived as the first campaign to go negative. And so we simply waited. And when we felt there was a response that had been elicited by the other side, then we went in with our negatives.

When you're working with a party committee you're removed from the candidate. That makes the tone more negative and, I think, is where the line gets crossed in terms of interpretation. And there's not the accountability because the candidate's not saying that's bullshit, I'm not going to say it.

Two others placed the blame on "third party committees." The reference was to an interest outside of the two contenders for office, not to a third political party:

I think the whole third party movement has made campaigns far more negative. If you look at the third party ads, 95% of them are negative. I think that has had a real effect on the tone. I think that goes back to the dorky campaign finance laws, which encourage negativity on the part of independent third parties.

I agree entirely. I think the third parties are doing the dirty work, and they're integrated. I mean, they're coordinated, although there are legal issues with some of that, but it allows the candidates to kind of emerge on the high ground while the third parties do the bad. . . .

Table 4-6 looks at these same data, analyzing differences among different kinds of campaigns. From the first two columns, one sees that House and Senate races do not differ greatly, except that Senate races, presumably those of challengers, tend to give more negative pictures of government institutions, officials, and policies. Races in which one incumbent faces another tend to talk more about specific issues than do

Table 4-6. Percentage of Campaign Communications Having Various Qualities,
By Type of Race

	House (%)	Senate (%)	Incumbent/ Incumbent (%)	Challenger/ Incumbent (%)	Open Seat (%)
High issue content	34	25	46	44	25
Highly relevant character information	17	22	12	25	16
Biased issue presentation	26	24	32	16	20
Specific issue statements	11	12	28	13	8
Negative overall tone	30	33	40	22	34
Negative about government institutions	7	23	10	19	7
Negative about government officials	11	22	30	20	9
Negative about government policies	12	24	16	20	13

Maximum $N = 1,263$.

Source: Campaign Advertising Data Set, 2002.

races in the other two categories, but those discussions tend to be more biased and the ads assume a more negative tone. Open seat races, those in which the winner is most in doubt, tend to be those with the least issue content, and the issue presentation that does exist is more biased than in campaigns in which an incumbent faces a challenger. The open seat campaigns also tend to be more negative than incumbent/challenger races.

Table 4-7 shows differences in the ways campaigns use various kinds of media pieces that contain the most discussion of issues; this characteristic follows naturally from the fact that direct mail pieces tend to be longer than any of the media examined. More than a quarter of the issue presentations using direct mail are perceived to be biased presentations of those concerns. What is also striking from these data is that radio advertisements are much more negative than those in any other medium. Television advertisements, the source of most campaign information for most voters – and the source that provides the perceptions of campaigns that most citizens form – appear to follow a predictable pattern. More than one-third of them are negative in tone; they are low in issue content; and, while only about one-sixth of them are critical of government institutions, officials, and policies, that percentage is higher than that found in the other media.

Our data set permits us to look at advertising appeals in considerable depth. For instance, one set of reformers feels that the quality of campaign

Table 4-7. Percentage of Campaign Communications Having Various Qualities, By Type of Communications

	Campaign Literature	Direct Mail	Radio Ads	Television Ads	Phone Calls
High issue content	24	41	20	27	20
Highly relevant character information	19	20	24	17	3
Biased issue presentation	25	28	35	24	19
Specific issue statements	6	14	6	10	3
Negative overall tone	6	28	50	36	36
Negative about government institutions	3	8	3	14	0
Negative about government officials	14	11	6	16	0
Negative about government policies	12	12	3	18	0

Maximum N = 1,263 observations.

Source: Campaign Advertising Data Set, 2002.

discourse will improve if candidates appear personally in their advertisements; the logic is that it is easier to have advertisements in which a surrogate attacks an opponent or in which issue positions are presented in a less than forthright way if the candidate does not make that presentation himself or herself.

In the campaign, we saw this reform addressing a real problem. Candidates appeared personally in nearly three-quarters of all of the advertisements we monitored (71 percent); opponents were portrayed in about one-third of the advertisements (34 percent). When candidates appeared personally in the ads, the ads were much less likely to be viewed as inaccurate or misleading (14 percent in the worse two categories on a 5-point scale, compared to 48 percent when the candidate did not appear), less likely to be viewed as strongly or somewhat negative in tone (15 percent when the candidate appeared personally compared to 67 percent when the candidate did not), and less likely to be viewed as biased (15–52 percent).

If the level of campaign discourse is to be raised, in order to give citizens more relevant information on which to base their votes, one would hope that the appeals made for voter support would be based on what the public can know about a candidate going into the voting booth, rather than on emotional feelings. Table 4-8 reveals that only 30 percent of the advertisements observed fell into either of the two highest categories based on cognitive appeal, while 43 percent were categorized as based

Table 4-8. Types of Appeals in Campaign Advertisements

	Cognitive Appeals (%)	Emotional Appeals (%)
1. Low	8	7
2.	24	24
3.	38	31
4.	26	27
5. High	4	16

$N = 1{,}263$ observations.
Source: Campaign Advertising Data Set, 2002.

Table 4-9. Percentage of Emotional and Cognitive
Appeals, By Party

	Republican (%)	Democrat (%)
High emotional appeal	48	38
High cognitive appeal	23	38

Maximum $N = 1{,}263$ observations.
Source: Campaign Advertising Data Set, 2002.

largely on emotional appeal. Table 4-9 shows that Republicans relied much more heavily on emotional appeals than on cognitive appeals, while the Democrats relied equally on the two.

Races in which two incumbents were running against each other were the only ones in which emotional and cognitive appeals were relied on equally. In each of the other types of races, emotional appeals were more prevalent than cognitive appeals. The disparity was most notable in open seat races (with 42 percent of the advertisements making highly emotional appeals and only 24 percent highly cognitive appeals.) Emotional appeals were more common than cognitive ones in all types of media examined. In this case, the disparity was most notable in television advertisements, with nearly half of those observed (48 percent) characterized as having highly emotional appeals and only about a quarter (27 percent) having highly cognitive appeals.

Cognitive appeals are largely based on factual statements made in the course of those appeals. Nearly four out of five of the examples of campaign discourse observed made factual claims. However, all factual claims are not of equal value. In recent years Ad Watches, carried on local television or in local newspapers for congressional elections, have monitored advertisements, often commenting on the accuracy of the claims made. Whereas once candidates might well have been fast and loose with the facts, in today's world they are more careful, in part out of fear of exposure.

In fact, our observers found nearly all of the advertisements analyzed (98 percent) to meet minimum tests of accuracy. However, technical accuracy does not necessarily give citizens the information they need to cast informed votes. Nearly a quarter of the advertisements observed were felt to be misleading (23 percent) and more than half failed to provide adequate context to evaluate the facts presented (56 percent). Only 10 percent of the observations were characterized as having provided full and accurate context. Nearly as many were felt to be too vague as to be worthwhile. No significant differences were observed by type of campaign, nor interestingly by type of media. The conclusion from these data is inescapable. In the media that campaigns produce and pay for themselves, they do not give the public the kind of information needed to cast informed votes.

According to the consultants we interviewed, the reason for this is simple. Issues do not win races; what wins a race is making your candidate look good and the other candidate look bad:

> If the polls says our numbers are going to jump if we go negative, then we push negative. And we say, we say, look, you know, you can run a very nice, pleasant campaign here. And you're going to lose. At the end of the day you can say you ran for congress and you lost. Or you can say, you can go out there with a sledge hammer because basically the polls says the only thing that's going to jump your campaign the ten points you need to jump it are these two negative messages. And personally in my firm, we will fight like hell to go negative, if we think that's the only way to win the race.

Similarly one could argue that emotional appeals, particularly negative emotional appeals, depend on how one characterizes one's opponent. More than a quarter of the advertisements mentioned that the opponent did not share the values of the district (28 percent); only slightly fewer claimed that the opponent was not honest (23 percent) or not caring (17 percent). Far fewer ads used character traits related to job performance. Only 7 percent of the advertisements we coded said that the opponent was not a strong leader and 3 percent said that he or she was inexperienced.

Table 4-10 presents three regression models analyzing the factors that contribute to advertisement tone, issue content, and issue bias. The

Table 4-10. Impact of Advertisement Characteristics on Advertisement Tone, Issue Content, and Issue Bias

	Advertisement Tone	Issue Content	Issue Bias
Candidate party	−0.20 (.08)**	0.25 (.06)***	−0.28 (.06)***
Open seat race	−0.088 (.08)	−0.22 (.06)***	0.004 (.06)
Candidate-sponsored ad	0.41 (.08)***	−0.36 (.06)***	−0.27 (.06)***
Candidate personally appears	1.54 (.09)***	0.19 (.07)**	−0.67 (.07)***
Degree of emotional appeals	−0.37 (.03)***	0.04 (.03)	0.29 (.03)***
Degree of cognitive appeals	−0.08 (.04)	0.69 (.03)***	−0.09 (.03)**
Constant	6.97 (.27)***	0.87 (.21)***	1.76 (.22)***
N	1,195	1,190	1,149
Adjusted R^2	.37	.36	.29

$^*p < .05; ^{**}p < .01; ^{***}p < .001.$
Note: The numbers shown are unstandardized regression coefficients, with standard errors in parentheses.
Source: Campaign Advertising Data Set, 2002.

factors that contributed to negative tones of advertisement were the advertisement not being sponsored by the candidate's own organization (i.e., advertisements sponsored by party committees or other interest groups), the candidate not appearing personally in the advertisement, the advertisement making a highly emotional appeal, and the advertisement having been run on behalf of a Democratic candidate. The last factor relates to the fact that the Democrats were the party in opposition. The emotional appeal is a tactical way to convey a negative message.

However, the first two findings are particularly important for a reform agenda and reflect a concern of those skeptical about campaign reforms. They argue, essentially, that reformers cannot concentrate on candidates and their campaigns as they most frequently do, because the candidate organizations are not the worst offenders. It appears quite likely that candidate organizations take the high road for strategic reasons. If surrogates will run the negative campaigns, the candidates themselves can appear to be above the fray while the negative message still gets out. Recall the comment from one of our interviews cited earlier:

I agree entirely. I think the third parties are doing the dirty work, and they're integrated. I mean, they're coordinated, although there are legal issues with some of that, but it allows the candidates to kind of emerge on the high ground while the third parties do the bad. . . .

Not going negative in advertisements in which the candidate appears personally follows from the same strategic thinking. If one goal of reform is to decrease the negative content of campaign discourse, effective means become apparent. The current law states that candidates must personally approve the messages sponsored by their campaign committees on the air. Perhaps it would be even more effective if candidates were encouraged to convey their own messages, both in the sense of sponsoring advertisement and delivering those messages from their own lips.

Factors linked to high issue content of advertisements were not very surprising. The positive tie to advertisements with high cognitive appeal is again a tactical question. Similarly Democrats run more issue-oriented advertisements because, in 2002, they were questioning the party in power. Open seat races tend to be more issue-oriented because two candidates, less well known by and large than the incumbent in a race in which one is running, are trying to create an impression of who they are and why they deserve support. Again, the important findings here are that issue content rises when the candidate's organization does not sponsor the advertisement and when the candidate delivers the message personally. Candidates want to be taken as serious people when seeking support, so they talk about the issues important to the public and to themselves. That kind of discourse should be encouraged. "Third party" organizations sponsor advertisements with high issue content, because they use those advertisements to run against a candidate, often in an unfair way, as we discuss below.

The most important findings regarding the bias of advertisements relate to the same factors as discussed above, for the opposite reasons. First, candidates do not want to appear personally in advertisements that appear to be biased; such appearances will only hurt their reputations. Better to leave that to third parties. Thus the finding that advertisements not sponsored by the candidates' organizations are the most biased. The remaining factors strongly linked to biased advertisements relate to how the ads are presented, not to why they are presented in that way.

Again, the lesson from the campaign advertisements for reformers seems clear. If one reads these data to state that the level of campaign discourse does not rise to an appropriate level, that campaigns are too negative, that content is insufficient for citizens to make informed judgments, reforms must be directed at the entire campaign process, not just at the activities of candidates and their own organizations. Campaigns can only be fully understood if one looks at all of the impressions that citizens receive. Only a portion of these comes from the candidate organizations or from the candidates themselves. Others – and some of the most important ones – come from third parties. Federal election law is clear that candidate organizations and party committees or interest groups cannot coordinate their activities. But only the most naïve observer denies that some coordination goes on. At the very least it appears that the candidates and the third parties agree that candidates can take the high road, not going negative, not attacking, not distorting, knowing that the third parties will do so on their behalf.

The consultants we interviewed all recognized this problem. One cited a specific example of a candidate running a television ad, taking it down, and then the same ad miraculously appearing under the sponsorship of an independent organization just days later. This consultant implied that no one seems to care about this collusion, not the candidates, not the parties, not the independent committees, and that the process cannot be cleaned up until that is recognized. Clearly he is a reform skeptic.

An unanswered question is the extent to which citizens understand this difference. Candidates may well be fooling themselves, thinking that they are not tainted because they do not deliver the negative message. Citizens look at a campaign as a whole. If Candidate X is under attack, only the most sophisticated political observer will note that the attack is from a congressional campaign committee, not from the candidate's opponent. But many citizens might note that they have not seen that opponent personally delivering a low blow. Consultants are not sure of the effect of this either. As one put it to us, "I'm not sure if the voters don't know where it's coming from or if they're so cynical or so smart that they just assume that everybody is working together. That if there's a third party, that they're not really a third party, that you guys know each other."

THE EFFECT OF VOLUNTARY CODES OF CONDUCT ON DISCOURSE:
THE CASE OF THE INSTITUTE FOR GLOBAL ETHICS

To look at reform impact, we compare discourse differences between the campaigns run in 5 contests in which candidates signed Institute for Global Ethics (IGE) voluntary codes of conduct and 22 elections in which they did not. IGE is a national reform organization financed by major foundations that has made a concerted effort to get congressional candidates to sign voluntary codes of conduct in which they pledge not to run negative ads or engage in deceptive or misleading styles of appeals. This organization obtained signed codes of conduct in three races (the second congressional district in Maine, the Maine U.S. Senate race, and the third congressional district in Ohio) and two in 2000 (the 17th district of Ohio and the 2nd district in Washington). We included the two districts from 2000 on the idea that if the reform effort is to be successful, there should be a carryover effect from year to year.

We make no claims that these five races are representative in any sense. For example, the two Maine races took place in a state with a tradition of clean campaigns. As early as 1982, two U.S. Senate candidates, George Mitchell (D), then serving as an appointed senator and seeking election to a full term in his own right, and David Emery, then a congressman seeking to move to the Senate, jointly urged outsiders not to come into the state with negative advertising because it was not in the Maine tradition. Maine candidates had signed voluntary codes for three election cycles prior to the 2002 midterm election. The second district in Washington turned out to be one of the least competitive of the campaigns we predicted to be competitive, in part at least because the challenger never mounted an effective challenge. The two Ohio races were for open seats. In Ohio 3, the Democrat never came as close to holding what had been a Democratic seat as analysts predicted. In Ohio 17, the seat was vacated by the convicted James Traficant, and both candidates wanted to demonstrate that they were different from Traficant and thus avoid any kind of negative image.

With those caveats, we compare IGE and non-IGE districts on type of communication tactics employed. As shown in Table 4-11, there were no discernible differences between the types of media run in these districts and the other campaigns. Forty-three percent of communications in IGE districts were television advertisements, compared to 46 percent in non-IGE races. Forty-four percent of the messages in IGE contests were direct mail, compared to 40 percent in non-IGE areas.

Table 4-12 compares the two sets of campaigns on three discourse dimensions: issue content, bias, and tone. Our goal was to see whether the IGE districts featured "better" discourse, according to the standards employed by reform organizations. In general, districts where IGE obtained signed conduct pledges had a higher issue content, were perceived to be less biased, and had a more positive tone than did the non-IGE campaigns. These differences were statistically significant at the .01 level, although bivariate association tests show that the relationships are quite weak.

Table 4-11. Types of Communications Observed in IGE
and Non-IGE Districts

	IGE Districts		Non-IGE Districts	
	Frequency	Percent	Frequency	Percent
Campaign literature	12	7	86	8
Direct mail	78	44	423	40
Radio ad	7	4	29	3
Television ad	76	43	498	46
Telephone call	3	2	35	3
Campaign speech	2	1	0	0
Total	178	101	1,071	100

Note: IGE districts are ME-2, OH-3, OH-17, WA-2, and ME Senate.
Source: Campaign Advertising Data Set, 2002.

Table 4-12. Summary Evaluations of Paid Media Content for IGE
and Non-IGE Districts

	Issue Content		Bias		Tone	
	IGE (%)	Non-IGE (%)	IGE (%)	Non-IGE (%)	IGE (%)	Non-IGE (%)
1. low/extreme bias/ strong negative	19	18	2	11	15	22
2.	12	23	9	18	5	10
3. medium/some bias/mixed	23	29	34	32	18	16
4.	32	21	33	26	19	15
5. high/no bias/strong positive	14	9	22	14	43	37
N	171	1,067	166	1,027	175	1,069
Kendall's tau-c	.073**		.116***		.061**	

*$p < .05$; **$p < .01$; ***$p < .001$.
Note: IGE districts are ME-2, OH-3, OH-17, WA-2, and ME Senate.
Source: Campaign Advertising Data Set, 2002.

Of course, it is possible that ad sponsorship (candidate vs. noncandidate) confounds the impact of reform. To see if that is the case, Table 4-13 breaks down IGE and non-IGE districts by whether the communications were sponsored by candidate or noncandidate organizations, such as political parties or interest groups. Two results are noteworthy.

Table 4-13. Percentage of Campaign Communications Having Various Characteristics, By Type of Sponsor for IGE and Non-IGE Districts

	Candidate		Noncandidate	
	IGE	Non-IGE	IGE	Non-IGE
High issue content	50 (109)	25 (529)	47 (59)	35 (507)
Highly relevant character information	23 (112)	21 (529)	12 (59)	15 (505)
Biased issue presentation	7 (106)	19 (509)	19 (57)	38 (500)
Specific issue statements	12 (113)	9 (526)	13% (60)	13 (502)
Negative overall tone	10 (112)	19 (529)	37 (60)	46 (509)
Negative about government Institutions	20 (113)	8 (529)	20 (61)	9 (497)
Negative about government officials	17 (113)	13 (525)	21 (61)	14 (506)
Negative about government policies	19 (113)	13 (529)	22 (59)	15 (510)

Values represent percentages; figures in parentheses are Ns.
Note: IGE districts are ME-2, OH-3, OH-17, WA-2, and ME Senate.
Source: Campaign Advertising Data Set, 2002.

First, non-candidate-sponsored advertisements in the IGE districts exhibited higher issue content, less bias, and a less negative tone than did those in non-IGE districts. This suggests that what we are observing did not only affect the candidates who signed the pledges, but also affected others involved in the race as well, political parties and interest groups.

Second, both candidate and non-candidate-sponsored appeals were more negative about government institutions, government officials, and government policies in the IGE districts than in the non-IGE districts. This finding leads one to ask whether those seeking to find ways to be critical simply found a different target in these races. Perhaps the conduct codes pushed campaign negativity in the direction of more generic targets, such as government and Congress, rather than the opposing candidate.

In short, our evaluation of the impact of IGE efforts in districts where they were successful at getting candidates to sign voluntary codes of campaign conduct is mixed. While these data show some encouraging signs, the low levels of association imply that any claims regarding significant improvement are weak at best. When one combines this finding with concern over the representativeness of the districts in which they were successful in having codes signed and their inability to reach agreements elsewhere, one has to be skeptical of systematic impact. For the vast majority of the country, this reform proposal was not implemented in any formal way, although some candidates might have informally agreed to respect such a practice. For that reason, it is hard to judge this specific reform as being very successful because so few congressional candidates agreed to its provisions.

Campaign Web Sites

Another dimension of campaign communications we examined involves electronic discourse. We had Web site observations in 21 of the 22 House districts and all 5 Senate campaigns. In most cases the Web sites were observed on a monthly basis, with changes noted between observations. The vast majority of observations were of the Democratic and Republican party candidates, but where relevant we also looked at Green, Libertarian, and Reform party candidates, as well as independents.

The first important question about Web sites as an emerging campaign tactic deals with ease of access. Campaign Web sites have existed for a number of years, but few campaign professionals shared the excitement that political scientists felt about their potential as a campaign tool.[14] By the midterm, however, as one of the participants in one of the consultants we interviewed said, "Your web site used to be an adjunct to your campaign, I think it's kind of where you start now."

However, the existence of a Web site does not guarantee its effectiveness. Citizens must know about the Web site and be able to access it easily. We gauged these questions in a number of different ways. A citizen can get to a link in a number of different ways. First, the campaign can lead the citizen to the link through publicizing the Web site. How often have you heard candidates get their Web sites link into every interview they give? How often does the Web site link appear in television ads or on campaign literature? Only 10 percent of the campaigns we analyzed advertised the Web address in all or the vast majority of their campaign material. Another third displayed that address in at least some of their material. But the other campaigns apparently felt that citizens interested in Internet access to their campaign could find the material themselves. The campaigns seemed not willing to share access data with the general public. Only four major party candidates had counting devices displayed on their Web sites; only one of these had registered more than 25,000 hits by the end of the campaign.

Table 4-14. Content of First Pages of Web Sites

Content Category	Percentage of Web Sites
Personal welcoming statement from the candidate	55
Party affiliation of the candidate	31
Candidate statement on issue positions	34
Media quotes on issue positions of candidate	23
Name of opponent	28
Criticism of opponent's issue positions	19
Criticism of opponent's performance	9
Advertisements by the campaign	19

Source: Campaign Web Site Data Set, 2002.

Unlike television advertising that confronts citizens while they are engaged in nonpolitical activities, or direct mail that arrives at a citizen's home uninvited (but, of course, must be read to be effective), Web-based campaigning must be accessed by interested citizens. If citizens are not led to the Web site by campaign advertising, most interested voters would look for a candidate's Web site using a search engine. When we entered candidates' names into widely used search engines, the campaign links came up as the first link cited 57.5 percent of the time. In over 90 percent of the cases, the link was among the top five. Thus, Internet savvy voters are able to find campaign Web sites if they go looking for them. And what information are campaigns trying to convey with their Web sites? Part of the answer should come from an examination of the first page of each Web site. Obviously, campaigns highlight the most important material first. Table 4-14 summarizes the first pages of the Web sites we examined.

The general impression that one gets from the first pages of the Web sites is that the campaign is making a positive statement for the candidate, but that statement does not seem very specific. Less than a third even mention the candidate's party affiliation. Only about a third have candidate statements on specific issues; about a fifth have media coverage of issues. Opponents are mentioned slightly more than one-quarter of the time, but even those references lack specificity. One-fifth of the sites provide links to campaign advertisements that appear in other media. The most common element, not surprisingly, is a welcoming statement from the candidate. Table 4-15 presents the content of these statements.

Table 4-15. Content of Welcoming Statements

Content Category	Percentage of Web Sites
Issue positions of the candidate	45
Statements about the candidate's character	36
Statements about values held by the candidate	50
Statements about policy accomplishments of the candidate	25
Statements about district service of the candidate	15
Party affiliation of the candidate	13
Encouragement to vote	17
Encouragement to participate in campaign	36
Criticism of opponent's issue positions	4
Criticism of opponent's character	3

Source: Campaign Web Site Data Set, 2002.

Web site welcoming statements, when used, provide the candidate with an opportunity to make a positive appeal for a citizen's support. Nearly half of the statements talk about specific issues; nearly half talk about the candidate's values. Many others talk about the candidate's character or his or her accomplishments based on which support is merited. Fewer talk about party affiliation or district or constituent service. And far fewer make the case for support in negative terms; fewer than 5 percent of the Web sites criticize opponents based on either issue positions or on character.

Web sites are used for strategic and tactical purposes. Among the strategic uses are the ability to reemphasize campaign themes and the ability to highlight those aspects of a candidate's record that seem advantageous. Among the tactical purposes are those best suited for high-speed electronic communication, for example, communicating with and coordinating volunteers. In addition, the Internet has been found to be a good recruitment tool. Table 4-16 lists the percentage of sites that provide links to various aspects of the campaign; the table also shows whether the link appears on the front page of the Web site or further into the site, a location that makes it more difficult for a visitor to access the link.

From this table, we can see that candidates used the sites for both the purposes mentioned above. Virtually all of the sites introduce the visitor to the candidate and discuss issue positions. Most also highlight news coverage of the campaign and reproduce press releases. Fewer go into great depth, for instance, by putting texts of speeches on the site (though one may be led to wonder how many of these candidates in fact gave prepared addresses that could have been so loaded).

Table 4-16. Links Found on Candidate Web Sites

	Front Page Links (%)	Other Links (%)	None (%)
Biography of candidate	97	0	3
Issue positions of candidate	84	5	12
Text of campaign speeches	15	4	81
News coverage of campaign	73	10	17
Press releases	54	19	27
Television or print ads of campaign	25	2	73
Campaign flyers and other material	10	4	86
Endorsements	47	12	40
Lists of supporters	13	12	75
Opportunity to volunteer	83	5	12
Opportunity to contribute	87	1	12
Sign up for e-mails	56	4	40
Candidate campaign schedules	30	14	56

Source: Campaign Web Site Data Set, 2002.

The sites are not used as frequently to reinforce campaign messages put forth on other media as one might expect. Only slightly more than one-third have links to television or print ads; only 14 percent allow the visitor to download campaign flyers or other materials. However, site designers want to give visitors the impression that they are in good company, highlighting the list of endorsements and campaign supporters.

What is most clear from this table, however, is the extent to which these sites are used as means to communicate with campaign supporters. Nearly 90 percent give the visitor the opportunity to volunteer or contribute; three in five give the visitor the chance to join an e-mail list. These links tend to be prominently displayed on the sites, almost always on the front page.

The conclusion that one is led to from the review of Web sites to this point is that this campaign medium is viewed as a way to communicate with supporters, not as a means to persuade undecided voters or to convert those favoring an opponent. And this strategy makes perfect sense. Who goes to a campaign Web site? Supporters go to see what is happening with their campaign. Volunteers are directed to the site to gather information about the campaign. Surely some supporters of an opponent go to the site, not to be convinced, but to find grist for later campaigning. Thus, it makes sense not to use the site to attack (as that would lead to counterattack). Similarly, we know that undecided voters during a campaign tend to be those least interested in the campaign.

Table 4-17. General Political Links Found on Campaign Web Sites

	Front Page Link (%)	Other Links (%)	None (%)
Voter registration information	33	2	65
Political party information	11	20	69
Government offices or organizations	5	22	73
Candidates in same party in other races	2	5	93
General news sources	24	21	56
Neutral information (e.g., Project Vote Smart)	1	5	94
Partisan political information (e.g., Americans for Democratic Action)	2	19	79

Source: Campaign Web Site Data Set, 2002.

Thus, they are the ones least likely to take the assertive steps needed to access any candidate's Web site. These voters want the campaign to come to them. They do not go to the campaign. And Web site designers understand this psychology. They do not use the site to convert, but rather to reinforce the support of those supporters they already have.

We can see this strategy in another way. Some reformers want campaigns to use their Web sites to inform voters, not just about the campaign sponsoring the Web site but about the electoral process in general. They see the Internet as the medium of the future to bring politics into the home in an easily accessible way. If campaign Web sites give voters general information, the level of information and participation of the voting populace will both improve. Table 4-17 presents data on more general political links that are found on some campaign Web sites.

The story could not be much more clear. Campaign Web site designers are not interested in providing neutral information or even information helpful to other candidates in their own party. They are not even interested in sending visitors to their site to other sites that might support their candidate. Why? Because those sites and other links on those sites are beyond their control. More sites provide front page links to voter registration information, but this choice is probably strategic as well. If one assumes that visitors to the site are likely to be supporters, it makes sense to help those unregistered to figure out what they must do to vote. If Web sites are to become a prominent medium for campaigning in the future, the evidence to date is that they will be used to shore up existing support and allow campaigns to communicate with the committed.[15]

CAMPAIGN COMMUNICATIONS THROUGH
THE NEWS MEDIA

Of course, citizens learn about campaigns through the news media as well as through media paid for by the campaigns. The divergence between paid media and free media is one often commented upon by those writing about campaigns. Campaigns like the control they have over the paid media; they control the message. However, they fully understand that free media, news coverage of campaigns, have a certain credibility that paid media lack. And many campaigns do not have large advertising budgets, so they must rely on free media coverage of the candidate to convey their message.

From the perspective of the public, news media can play several roles. News coverage, free media to the candidates, could enhance the substantive content of information reaching the citizens; it could be used to call into account those who are running negative campaigns. In short, an alert, attentive, and concerned media covering a campaign could play a key role in enhancing the level of the political discourse reaching the public.

THE NEWS MEDIA DATA SET

To explore the role of the news media in the 27 competitive districts that we studied in-depth, the independent scholars working in the districts and states gathered detailed news media data. One part involved careful monitoring of all news stories on a series of specific days designated throughout the campaigns. In addition, those monitoring these campaigns summarized the news coverage they observed during specific weeks throughout the campaign season. As a result of coding these observations, we have summaries of 522 individual newspaper stories, 100 television stories, and 639 weekly summaries.[16]

CONTENT OF NEWS COVERAGE   What one finds in examining news coverage depends in large part on one's expectations. What can one legitimately expect a news station to convey about a campaign? Ideally, one would like to see in-depth stories about the candidates, their stands on issues, comparisons between and among candidates, and analyses of the claims that candidates are making. But reality never reaches this ideal – and it does not do so for some very legitimate reasons.

Let's start by looking at the presidential campaign. One would hope that news organizations would devote a good deal of time and resources to covering the race for the presidency; and they do. But still, many are dissatisfied with the extent of the coverage, with its depth. We hear frequent complaints about the emphasis on the horse race, with too little attention to the substance of the issues. We hear complaints that journalists, particularly television journalists, oversimplify, that they accept and pass on stereotypic views of a campaign. And, of course, we hear complaints about pack journalism, that the leading journalists tell one story and everyone else follows; the conventional wisdom is defined by a few and accepted by the many.

To a large extent this picture is true of television coverage of presidential campaigns, and even of coverage by some newspapers. But to an equally large extent, this picture of a news media not serving the public is overstated. The in-depth stories are written; they are aired. The question is who is watching them. Who is paying attention? Journalists must write to their audience. They are aware that most viewers and readers do not spend hours looking at in-depth comparisons of candidates' views. So they do present those comparisons, but they also summarize them – and it is often these summaries that are caricatured. It is also often these summaries that are viewed or read by the average citizen.

Is that the fault of the news media? Of the journalists covering a campaign? We think the blame must be shared. But remember, to this point we have been talking about presidential campaigns. The nation's news networks and major newspapers and news magazines, with multimillion dollar budgets, invest heavily in covering these quadrennial events. And so they should, given the importance of a presidential election for the entire nation, the audience for these media. And even with the national attention and vast budgets, media are criticized for the quality of their coverage.

Now go down to the level of a campaign for the U.S. Senate or one of the House of Representatives. Only rarely do any of these campaigns draw national attention, and then the attention is not sustained. Rather, they are covered by a state's media or local media, depending on the race; and that is appropriate. But if the national media have difficulty attracting citizen attention to in-depth stories about presidential campaigns, think of the problem facing the news organizations covering the campaigns with which we are concerned. And they must do so operating under constraints that dwarf those of national organizations, severe constraints in terms of money, staff, and time or space available.

Let us focus for a moment on campaigns for the House of Representatives, as most of the competitive races we studied were House races. In urban settings, newspapers' and television stations' audiences reside in more than one congressional district. At the extreme, more than 30 Members of Congress and 6 U.S. senators are covered by the New York City media market. In other large cities, with large daily papers and television stations with serious news organizations, the multiple district problem also exists, though to a lesser extent. How can these papers and stations cover all of the races in their areas? The answer is that they do not have the ability to do so adequately. The news hole is too small and must be divided. The staff is stretched too thin to have detailed knowledge of all the candidates.

The opposite problem exists in rural settings. Whereas all of Maine contains only two congressional districts, the media still cannot devote adequate resources to cover these races. In this case, the problem is resource availability. Newspapers and television stations in rural areas run on small budgets. Reporters, who are often undertrained and underpaid, are also often overworked. They must cover all sorts of stories over a vast geographic expanse. The "political reporter" per se does not exist. One reporter covers congressional politics, state politics, and often local politics. Congressmen and U.S. senators in these states are often celebrities; they are covered as such, not with a critical eye but with one filled with respect for the office and often the incumbent.

Given these constraints, we should not expect the coverage of even the competitive campaigns we studied to make up for lack of substance found in the paid media. We would hope, however, that the tone of the free media coverage and its balance would enhance the level of discourse.

One of the frequent complaints about campaign advertisements is that little can be said in a 30-second ad. Do news stories permit more depth? We do not find evidence that gives much hope. Nearly 65 percent of the television news stories were 1 minute in length or less; over 62 percent of the newspaper stories were of less than 500 words (see Table 4-18). It is difficult to convey much substance in stories of these lengths, just as difficult as it is in a 30-second commercial.

As mentioned earlier, another frequent criticism of news coverage of campaigns is that the stories talk about only the campaigns themselves, not about the issues of the campaign. Nearly two-thirds of the more than 600 stories coded dealt only with the campaigns as such, not the issues; nearly 90 percent of the television stories – almost all of which appeared late in the electoral season – were "horse race" and campaign strategy stories. In contrast only about one in six stories dealt with policy issues, in which the position of one or more of the candidates on specific issues was discussed. Only one-tenth dealt with the performance of incumbents

Table 4-18. Length of Campaign News Stories

Media Type	Length of Story	Percentage of Stories
Television stories	Less than 15 sec	13
	15–29 sec	31
	30 sec to 1 min	22
	Over 1 min	25
	Not sure/Web monitoring	10
		$N = 88$
Newspaper stories	Less than 200 words	26
	200–499 words	37
	500–699 words	21
	700–899 words	10
	Over 900 words	7
		$N = 538$

Note: Length of television and newspaper news stories is based on the approximate length of the story. Percentages may not sum to 100 due to rounding.
Source: Campaign News Media Data Set, 2002.

Table 4-19. Level of Substance Provided by Campaign News Coverage

	Percentage of Stories with Level of None or Low	
Area of Coverage	Democratic Candidates	Republican Candidates
Issue positions	72 (616)	74 (614)
Past record	88 (612)	87 (606)
Qualifications for office	91 (609)	94 (604)
Personal characteristics	91 (611)	92 (604)

Values represent percentages; figures in parentheses are *N*s.
Note: Responses to the original categories of none and low were combined to produce the percentages displayed in this table.
Source: Campaign News Media Data Set, 2002.

in office. When our observers were asked to evaluate the quality of the news coverage provided in individual stories, only 8.5 percent of the stories were coded in the highest category, "coverage provides ample information"; 27.9 percent felt that the story fell into the lowest category, "coverage lacks appropriate information." As Table 4-19 shows, nearly three-quarters of the stories provided no information on candidate issue positions or very little; nearly seven out of eight did not discuss their past records in any depth. Over 90 percent failed to go into detail on candidate qualifications or relevant personal characteristics.

The first conclusion from examining campaign coverage is that it was short, campaign-oriented, not issue-oriented, and that it provided little relevant information to citizens as they sought to decide among competing candidates in critical races.

In order to appreciate the type of coverage received, we also asked observers to code the depth of issue coverage of the stories they were analyzing. The scale in this case went from "very little contextual information or discussion" to "great deal of information about policy problems and proposed solutions"; 52 percent of the stories were coded in the lowest two categories, showing lack of depth of coverage, while only 16 percent were in the top two categories.

In addition, we asked whether the tone of the stories was positive or negative, generally and as they pertained to specific substantive items, like policy positions and character. For virtually every question the modal answer was neutral, if one discounted the high percentage who responded "not covered." On the one hand, one could interpret this finding positively: The media were not biased and did not contribute to the negativity of campaigning. On the other hand, one could interpret the finding negatively: The media did not go into enough depth to state any opinions on the substance of the campaign or the issues in the campaign. Given that the "not covered" response exceeded 70 percent on all but two questions, we opt for the latter interpretation.

Finally, we asked for an overall assessment of the quality of the stories on three criteria – overall quality of the coverage, depth of the issue coverage, relevance of the character information provided in the story (see Table 4-20). The stories were rated overwhelmingly low on the overall quality of the coverage and on the depth of issue coverage. The ratings on the relevance of character coverage were more balanced, but the low "N" reflects the fact that most stories did not deal with character coverage at all.

These assessments are based on individual news stories throughout the campaign. However, the public's knowledge comes from the accumulation of stories. The reason we asked our observers to monitor stories over weeklong periods (including the last 2 weeks of the campaign) was to assess the cumulative impact.

One important benchmark is whether or not a media outlet has regular coverage of election campaigns. The assumption is that reporters whose regular beats involve election coverage are more likely to be knowledgeable analysts of those campaigns than are reporters who cover campaigns

Table 4-20. Summary Evaluations of Campaign News Coverage

Evaluative Ranking	Overall Quality of Coverage (%)	Depth of Issue Coverage (%)	Relevance of Character Coverage (%)
Low	54	61	37
Moderate	21	19	28
High	25	19	36
N	625	519	323

Note: For overall quality of coverage, depth of issue coverage, and relevance of character coverage, the original 5-point scales have been collapsed into 3-point scales, with original responses of 1 and 2 being classified as low, original responses of 3 as moderate, and original responses of 4 and 5 as high. Percentages may not sum to 100 due to rounding.
Source: Campaign News Media Data Set, 2002.

Table 4-21. Extent of Regular Campaign Coverage by Media Outlets

	Newspapers		Television Stations	
	Regular Coverage (%)	No Regular Coverage (%)	Regular Coverage (%)	No Regular Coverage (%)
House races	20	80	5	95
N	255	128		
Senate races	20	80	13	87
N	85	47		

Source: Campaign News Media Data Set, 2002.

only rarely. Very few Senate campaigns and even fewer congressional district campaigns were regularly covered (see Table 4-21). As is not surprising, television media outlets covered campaigns even less regularly than did newspapers. Slightly more than one-third of those stations or newspapers that did provide regular campaign coverage did so on a daily basis; nearly half provided only weekly updates until the final week of the campaign.

Our observers' assessments of the quality of coverage, gauging from a week-to-week view rather than from evaluating individual articles, were no more positive. More than half of the news sources were deemed to be of low quality, another quarter of moderate quality, with approximately the same number of high quality. It is difficult to come to a sanguine view of the role of the press in informing the public about electoral campaigns when one examines these analyses. Press coverage, whether observers are looking at individual stories or all of the stories over a period of time, is judged to be poor.

Only a few media outlets received high grades when industry leaders were probed on this subject during our interviews with them. One consultant praised the media in a Midwestern city, claiming, "They ran a series on social security that spelled out the differences between the parties in terms the public could understand. Everywhere else, reporters seemed unable to figure out what the real issue was, much less to explain it to anyone else." In praising the media in one market, this consultant damned the rest of the coverage he observed.

Another one of those we interviewed summed up his feelings about the role of the media in this way:

> I really agree that the quality of reporting on local campaigns is so poor these days that if you want to get better interesting campaigns, you'd have better writing and reporting on campaigns at the local level. President, Presidential level, it's fine. Local level, it's awful.

None of the other interviewees disagreed with this view; many echoed these comments. The conclusion that citizens cannot get the information they need to make rational decisions on congressional and senatorial elections from the electronic media is beyond doubt. In a minority of markets it may be possible to become adequately informed from the print media, but even this requires considerable citizen effort. While the reasons for the relatively poor coverage of congressional and senatorial campaign – from the point of view of the media – are easy to understand, the conclusion remains inescapable – and that bodes ill for an effective electoral process with discourse that informs the electorate.

CONCLUSION

If the standard is that campaigns should be civil and substantive, that the efforts by campaigns and the reporting by the media should provide the voters with information so that they can make informed, rational decisions about which candidates to support, it is difficult not to judge that the campaigns observed in the most competitive congressional and senatorial races failed to make the grade. Neither the incentives driving campaign managers nor the best efforts of reformers led to a campaign discourse like that envisioned by reform optimists.

Our academic observers were asked to generalize about the campaigns they studied. Most concluded that substantive discussion of policy alternatives was not on the table. Issues were not stressed by candidates; the media did not fill the void. With few exceptions, such as a newspaper series on health care policy and the implications of the two candidates' views in one district, citizens made judgments, even in the most competitive districts, based on superficial coverage of the pressing issues of the day.

But questions still remain. Who is to blame, if blame should be passed out? Is there more that could be done? Have we observed the failure of specific reform efforts or is this lack of success due to more fundamental misconceptions about how to reform the campaign process? Before we turn to these questions, we will examine the impact that the reforms that were attempted had on public perceptions.

FIVE

Impact on Public Responses

Voters play a crucial role in campaign reform. They are the objects of persuasion and mobilization, and the people who are on the receiving end of political advertisements, news coverage, debates, mailings, phone calls, Web sites, and speeches. Efforts to make the electoral system work better center on how citizens feel about the political process. Without some positive impact on the general public, campaign reform cannot be judged effective. It is not enough for consultants, candidates, and reporters to view proposed remedies as an improvement. Rather, citizens must see a difference in how elections function.

These objectives are difficult to achieve because there long has been a culture of cynicism and dissatisfaction in the United States. Citizens do not trust the government in Washington to do what is right.[1] Following Watergate, Vietnam, economic stagflation, Iran-Contra, the House bank scandal, and Monica Lewinsky, voters believe that politicians are out for themselves and are not likely to represent the public interest.

This chapter looks at how voters have responded to campaign reform proposals and whether changes are associated with making citizens feel better about the system. Using the results of our national public opinion survey, we examine voter opinions about campaign reform and the election. If there were debates, forums, and candidate pledges to avoid negative campaigning in the person's local congressional district, was there any association with citizen impressions of campaign tone, issue discussion, and knowledge of the candidates? In addition, do reforms bear any relationship to levels of citizen engagement in the campaign and feelings of satisfaction with the election outcome?

Similar to the doubts of reform skeptics, our results show that there are weak ties between the existence of these reform activities and perceptions of improved campaign tone, knowledge of the candidates, or satisfaction with the electoral outcome. The only factors showing a significant link with reform were in citizens believing that policy discussion improved over the course of the campaign and people who reported that their level of campaign interest went up. As demonstrated in this chapter, it takes a lot more than incremental reforms to make citizens feel better about the contemporary political process.

THE CULTURE OF VOTER CYNICISM AND DISSATISFACTION

There are many reasons why Americans mistrust their government and are dissatisfied with the quality of campaigns. As pointed out in the previous chapter, news coverage leaves a lot to be desired. At election time, television stations and other media outlets devote scant attention to political contests and focus more on drama than on substance. And in terms of the governing process, reporters sometimes focus on background or character issues as opposed to the future direction of the country.[2]

Candidates fare little better in the eyes of citizens. Voting statistics show citizens do not feel very engaged in the electoral process. They complain about excessive negativity in the campaign and candidates who duck important issues. Many citizens believe campaigns have become too shrill and meaningless in content. Rather than pointing out substantive differences that educate the public, some contenders sling mud at the opposition and distract voters with nonsubstantive campaign appeals.[3]

One can put this cynicism into a context of failed or flawed performance in governance over a long period of time. There have been lengthy periods of unsatisfactory performance that has heightened citizen dissatisfaction with the political system. President Lyndon Johnson's lies about the progress of the war in Vietnam and President Richard Nixon's deceit and obstructionism in the Watergate scandal undermined the fundamental bases of public trust in government.[4]

The leak of the Pentagon Papers in 1971 to various newspapers was a shocking development to the American people. These government documents showed that although President Johnson had continued to assure the American people throughout his presidency that progress was being made in Indochina, he had known that the war in Vietnam was not going well and had gotten advice from numerous experts that the United States needed an exit strategy.[5] In effect, the Pentagon Papers showed that the president had not been forthcoming with the American people.

Following closely on the heels of Vietnam was, perhaps, the most egregious example of government malfeasance. After a very close electoral victory in 1968, and amid growing public sentiment against the war in Vietnam, President Nixon was deeply worried – perhaps paranoid – about his prospects for reelection in 1972. Given the president's misgivings about his electoral prospects, the Committee to Reelect the President orchestrated an early morning break-in of the Democratic Party's national headquarters at the Watergate hotel and office complex to copy internal files about Democratic strategies for the upcoming election. Unfortunately for President Nixon, the burglars were caught by a security guard and were arrested by Washington, DC, police.

Investigative reporting by heretofore unknown *Washington Post* reporters Bob Woodward and Carl Bernstein slowly uncovered the links between the burglars and president's reelection committee. Although the president and members of his administration denied any wrongdoing or prior knowledge of the break-in, congressional and media investigations discovered they were not being honest. After 2 years of public denial and constant obstruction by the president and many of his staff and following the Supreme Court's determination that the president had to turn over the secretly taped recordings of conversations in the Oval Office to Congress, the public discovered that Nixon and his top aides were aware of the plans and had financed key actions by the burglars. The resulting outcry forced Nixon to resign his presidency on August 8, 1974.

The loss of confidence in government following Vietnam and Watergate was far-reaching. According to one scholar, the decline in trust for the presidency was about 50 percent across every major subgroup of citizenry.[6] As a result of Watergate and a dismal economy in the 1970s, Americans became less confident in the president's ability to perform his duties, became much more likely to believe that the office of the presidency needed serious reform, and were more likely to feel powerless about the political process.[7]

In the 1970s, the country was hurt by the combination of high unemployment and inflation (leading to the term stagflation).[8] This led not just to poor ratings for individual officeholders, such as then President Jimmy Carter, but citizen unhappiness with the entire political system. Indeed, dissatisfaction with Carter's performance on the economy and in foreign policy led to a sense that things were not going well in America. This discontent with government and its related institutions, such as the nation's political parties, resulted in increasingly cynical public attitudes.[9] President Carter's infamous "malaise" speech, which called attention to the assorted difficult issues facing the country during this period, did little to assure his fellow Americans and contributed to a general sense of unhappiness with the system.

The Iran hostage crisis, and the failed rescue attempt that resulted in the deaths of eight U.S. servicemen, cemented the view that America was no longer the great power of World War II. Confirming what the American people had feared about their country during the preceding Vietnam years, the hostage takeover signified that the United States was an impotent and declining nation.

President Ronald Reagan briefly restored some confidence in government (mainly due to a rising economy), but his poor judgment in the Iran-Contra scandal further weakened citizen confidence in government. Determined to stop the advance of Communism worldwide, the president advanced the Reagan doctrine, which stated unequivocal U.S. opposition to continued Soviet aggression and deemed American support of freedom fighters around the globe as essential to the maintenance of U.S. national security. The Sandinista government in Nicaragua was viewed as an attempt by the Soviet Union to penetrate the Western Hemisphere beyond Fidel Castro's Cuba. Knowing there was no public support for direct action to counter this threat, the administration opted to fund the guerilla activities of opponents to the Sandinista regime – dubbed the "Contras" – as a way to check Soviet advancement in the region.[10]

Unfortunately for the Reagan administration, the Democratically controlled House and a closely divided Senate voted to end military aid to the Contras. Rather than accept this outcome, the Reagan administration attempted to circumvent congressional restrictions by the covert sale of arms to Iran in exchange for a commitment by the Islamic state to put serious pressure on Iranian-funded terrorists who held captive several Americans in the Middle East. The administration used a portion of the profits from the arms sales to fund the Contras.[11] When news of the scandal broke, not only did it damage Reagan's standing but it also deepened public cynicism toward and resentment against other public institutions.

Most recently, personal scandals and lifestyle embarrassments have plagued several prominent politicians, such as dozens of congressmen who were caught bouncing checks at the House bank with no consequences, former House Speaker Newt Gingrich, and most especially former President Bill Clinton.[12] When then Arkansas Governor Clinton ran for the Democratic nomination for president, allegations about marital infidelity surfaced as Gennifer Flowers claimed to have had a 12-year affair with the governor. Although this scandal did not derail his electoral bid, his presidency was plagued by a number of different accusations: an Arkansas land development deal referred to as Whitewater, a sexual harassment lawsuit brought by Paula Jones, a former hotel worker in Arkansas, who claimed that Clinton had exposed himself to her, and an affair with White House intern Monica Lewinsky.[13]

As the Lewinsky allegation broke, Clinton forcefully denied the charges. First Lady Hillary Rodham Clinton defended her husband and called the complaint a "vast right-wing conspiracy" designed to destroy her husband's presidency. Although President Clinton testified under oath that he "did not have sexual relations with that woman, Ms. Lewinsky," the evidence portrayed another story. The smitten Lewinsky had saved a semen-stained dress from an encounter with the president, and DNA evidence proved without a doubt that the president had engaged in an improper relationship with the young intern.[14]

The 2000 election did little to restore public confidence in government. After a competitive campaign, the election night produced an outcome in Florida that was so close that it took 6 weeks to resolve the legal issues associated with the balloting. In the end, a U.S. Supreme Court decision gave Florida to Bush and with it a majority of the Electoral College. Democrats cried foul and accused Republicans of "stealing" the election. The disputed nature of this contest polarized the country and harmed citizen trust in the electoral system.

Political polarization has continued throughout Bush's two terms in office. In his first term, Bush and congressional Republicans cut taxes and launched wars in Afghanistan and Iraq; and during his second term, a top aide to Vice President Richard Cheney was forced to resign following an indictment for perjury related to leaking the name of a CIA operative to the press and House Majority Leader Tom DeLay was indicted on ethics grounds and voluntarily resigned his seat.

The cumulative impact of each of these political and electoral events over the past 30 years contributed to a general unhappiness among Americans with how politicians, judges, and reporters were performing their jobs. Given the ups and downs of campaigns, media coverage, advertisements, the economy, domestic policy, and foreign affairs, it is not surprising that with a few exceptions, voter turnout has been low (see Table 4-1). Many citizens no longer believe that politicians represent the average person, but instead kowtow to unions, trial lawyers, and big corporate interests. With media coverage increasingly emphasizing personal scandal and campaign negativity, it has become harder and harder to engage citizens in the act of governance.[15] People feel disenchanted with the electoral process, which continues to undermine public confidence in American democracy.

THE LINK BETWEEN REFORM AND IMPROVED CAMPAIGNS

Given the persistent nature of citizen dissatisfaction, one of the key questions about campaign reform is whether proposed changes are linked to improved public feelings about the campaign and assessments of the political system. The hope of reformers is that by changing campaign finance laws, improving media performance, and altering campaign practices, citizens will regain confidence in the political system and feel better about the electoral process. If there is not some association between campaign reforms and more positive feelings about the campaign and the political system, an important tenet of the reform effort is undermined.

To investigate this linkage, we examined voter impressions about the congressional race by districts in which voters saw reforms taking place and areas where they did not occur. We looked at four specific reforms: debates, issues forums, conduct codes, and pledges to avoid negative campaigning. These represent major initiatives of reformers in recent election cycles and attempts to improve contemporary campaigns. In particular, we wanted to know whether districts where reforms were visible were associated with voter perceptions that the campaign was conducted with a more positive tone and more issue discussion and led to a greater knowledge about the candidates running for office.

As noted in earlier chapters, we cannot prove causality with these data. We compare voter perceptions of districts with and without reforms to see whether there is any association with impressions of "good" election outcomes. If there is an association, it suggests the possibility that reform may be responsible, subject of course to the mediating effects of other forces. However, if there is no linkage, it casts doubt on reformer arguments about the beneficial aspects of their initiatives.

In looking at the analysis shown in Table 5-1, it is clear that there was not much evidence of improved campaigns arising from formal debates. Having debates involving both major candidates for Congress

Table 5-1. Voter Impressions of Campaign by Existence of
Formal Debates Between Candidates

	Debates	No Debates
Overall tone more negative	40 (120)	31 (74)
Less issue discussion	50 (148)	53 (126)
Pleased with result	54 (159)	54 (129)
Knew name of winning candidate	49 (144)	54 (129)
Followed House race very closely	35 (103)	30 (71)

Values represent percentages; *N* for subcategory is in parentheses.
Source: National Public Opinion Survey, 2002.

Table 5-2. Voter Impressions of Campaign by Existence of Issue Forums

	Issue Forums	No Issue Forums
Overall tone more negative	36 (103)	36 (76)
Less issue discussion	47 (133)	59 (126)
Pleased with result	55 (155)	53 (112)
Knew name of winning candidate	54 (152)	48 (102)
Followed House race very closely	41 (115)	23 (48)

Values represent percentages; *N* for subcategory is in parentheses.
Source: National Public Opinion Survey, 2002.

was not associated with better campaign tone, more issue discussion, or greater voter knowledge. Fifty percent of voters living in districts where debates occurred felt the election had less issue discussion than previous years, while 53 percent of voters residing in areas that had no congressional debates agreed. There also were few differences between areas having and not having debates by whether voters knew the name of the winning candidate, followed the race very closely, or believed that campaign conduct codes were very important or effective.

We also compared districts that had issue forums for the major candidates with those that did not. As shown in Table 5-2, there were some notable differences. Voters in congressional districts with issue forums were more likely than those not in such districts to believe that there had been more issue discussion (34 to 21 percent) than in past years and to say that they had followed the congressional race very closely (40 to 22 percent).

Table 5-3 contrasts districts where there were and were not specific codes of conduct that guided the candidates. Voters in districts with such

Table 5-3. Voter Impressions of Campaign by Existence of Code of Conduct

	Conduct Codes	No Conduct Codes
Overall tone more negative	35 (73)	38 (93)
Less issue discussion	45 (92)	59 (146)
Campaign ads hurt process	58 (120)	68 (167)
Pleased with result	56 (116)	51 (126)
Knew name of winning candidate	50 (103)	50 (122)
Followed House race very closely	38 (78)	29 (71)
Conduct code is very important	55 (113)	49 (121)
Candidate abided very well by conduct pledge	19 (40)	0 (0)
Aware of IGE reform effort	24 (50)	16 (39)
Conduct code very effective	22 (45)	24 (59)

Values represent percentages; N for subcategory is in parentheses.
Source: National Public Opinion Survey, 2002.

codes were about as likely as those living in areas without codes to think the campaign was negative. However, they were more likely to feel that there was discussion of the issues and less likely to feel that ads had hurt the political process. There was no difference in knowing the name of the winning congressional candidate, but voters residing in areas with a code of conduct were more likely to say that they had closely followed their local House race. In regard to campaign reform, voters who said there were codes of conduct were more likely than those not living in such districts to believe such a code was very important (55 to 49 percent). These voters also were more aware of IGE reform efforts (24 percent) than those living in districts without such codes (16 percent).

To examine the impact of candidate pledges to avoid negative tactics, Table 5-4 shows the results for voters who reside in congressional districts where candidates took a pledge. There were no major differences between districts where there was and was not such a pledge. For example, while 35 percent of citizens living in places where candidates took a pledge thought the campaign was more negative than in the past, 37 percent who lived in places where there was no candidate pledge on negativity agreed. Similarly, there was little difference between the two types of districts in voter knowledge of the winning candidate's name or in beliefs about the importance of a campaign conduct code.

However, there were some clear differences between these cohorts. For instance, 57 percent of citizens living in areas where there were no pledges believed the campaign had generated less issue discussion while only 45 percent of those living elsewhere agreed. Additionally, in districts

Table 5-4. Voter Impressions of Campaign by Existence of Pledge to Avoid
Negative Campaigning

	Candidate Pledges	No Candidate Pledges
Overall tone more negative	35 (75)	37 (102)
Less issue discussion	45 (98)	57 (157)
Campaign ads hurt process	64 (139)	63 (173)
Pleased with result	55 (118)	54 (149)
Knew name of winning candidate	51 (110)	50 (138)
Followed House race very closely	38 (82)	29 (80)
Conduct code is very important	50 (107)	51 (142)
Candidate abided very well by conduct pledge	17 (21)	17 (9)
Conduct code very effective	19 (41)	25 (69)

Values represent percentages; *N* for subcategory is in parentheses.
Source: National Public Opinion Survey, 2002.

where there were pledges, voters were more likely than their counterparts (38 to 29 percent) to say that they had closely followed the campaign.

To summarize, this analysis demonstrates that there were some relationships between campaign reform and improved issue discussion, but the linkages were neither strong nor consistent. There were lots of cases where there were no differences in campaign conduct between districts having or not having particular reforms. And in some cases, our results ran contrary to the hopes and expectations of reformers. At least at the preliminary level, these findings do not generate a lot of confidence in the ability of reforms to improve citizen feeling about contemporary campaigns.

A MULTIVARIATE ASSESSMENT OF THE IMPACT OF CAMPAIGN REFORM

The preceding section examined the link at the bivariate level between campaign reform and voter impressions of the election. However, it is important to determine whether these results hold up once multivariate controls are introduced into the analysis. There are a variety of other factors beyond reform that affect how Americans view candidates and campaign conduct. We need to incorporate those features in our analysis to see how they affect the association with reform.

In order to examine the strength of those relationships, we ran 15 regressions to test the association between the presence and absence of each reform initiative (debates, issue forums, conduct codes, and pledges to avoid negativity plus a summary reform index) on three measures of campaign conduct (campaign tone, issue discussion, and voter knowledge of candidates). We looked at the association of each reform separately because few congressional districts had all the changes present at the same time.[16]

In addition to studying the impact of each individual proposal, we created an overall campaign reform index consisting of the sum of these four campaign reforms. This index measured whether 0, 1, 2, 3, or 4 of these reform activities occurred in the local congressional district. This enabled us to investigate the cumulative impact of reform and to see how districts with more extensive implementation compared to areas with less adoption.

To ensure our results were not artifacts of differences in the types of people who hold particular views about the midterm campaign, we controlled for party, ideology, sex, age, region, income, education, and race. Other studies have found each of these controls to be related to political views and impressions about campaigns.[17] Party and ideology are related to a variety of political impressions held by voters. The others are demographic factors that condition how people acquire and process information about the political world.

Since campaign tone (positive, same as before, or negative) and issue discussion (more, same as before, or less) were measured through variables having three categories, we used ordinary least squares to estimate effects. However, we employed logistic regression for knowledge of the winning candidate's name because that variable was dichotomous (voters either knew or did not know the name).

Most of the 15 regressions did not produce significant associations between reform and campaign discourse. Having issue forums was not associated with more positive campaign rhetoric. None of the reform activities displayed any significant relationship with voter knowledge. It did not matter whether there were debates, issue forums, or candidate pledges; not a single one of these reform efforts was associated with boosting voter knowledge of the candidate's name. Candidate pledges to avoid negative campaigning were not associated with higher levels of policy discussion.

Indeed, only 4 of the 15 regressions showed significant links to reform (see Table 5-5). However, holding debates was significant, but in the *opposite* direction to that desired by reformers. Districts with debates tended to feature a more negative discussion, probably as a result of the

Table 5-5. Regression Results for Campaign Reform on Voter Views About Campaign Tone and Issue Discussion

	Tone	Issue Discussion	Issue Discussion	Issue Discussion
Formal debates	−.15 (.07)*	—	—	—
Issue forums	—	.32 (.09)***	—	—
Code of conduct	—	—	.21 (.10)*	—
Summary campaign reform index	—	—	—	.09 (.04)*
Party identification	−.09 (.05)	−.09 (.06)	−.11 (.06)	−.13 (.07)
Ideology	−.05 (.05)	−.11 (.07)	−.17 (.07)*	−.11 (.08)
Sex	−.17 (.07)*	−.03 (.09)	−.19 (.10)*	−.12 (.11)
Age	.01 (.01)	.007 (.02)	.007 (.02)	.006 (.02)
Income	.01 (.02)	.06 (.03)*	.05 (.03)	.08 (.03)**
Education	.04 (.02)*	.03 (.03)	.03 (.03)	−.003 (.03)
Race	−.11 (.10)	.18 (.12)	.15 (.13)	.30 (.14)*
South/non-South	.16 (.08)*	−.16 (.10)	.28 (.10)**	.25 (.11)*
Constant	2.57 (.31)***	1.23 (.40)**	1.71 (.39)***	1.08 (.49)*
Adjusted R^2	.05	.06	.08	.08
F statistic	3.18***	3.48***	4.22***	3.48***
N	405	373	343	273

*$p < .05$; **$p < .01$; ***$p < .001$.
Note: The numbers are unstandardized regression coefficients, with standard errors in parentheses. The number of asterisks indicates the statistical significance of the coefficient.
Source: National Public Opinion Survey, 2002.

combative nature of many congressional debates. This is not the outcome that reform-oriented activists would want.

On the other hand, there were strong and statistically significant positive relationships between two of the specific reforms and the level of policy discussion in the campaign. The existence of issue forums and situations where at least one candidate took a specific pledge to abide by a code of conduct in running the race showed significant links to voter impressions about the amount of issue discussion during the electoral cycle. When one of these reforms was present during the campaign, voters believed there was more policy discussion in the race. Similarly, the campaign reform index regression shows a significant relationship between the number of reforms present in the district and the level of policy discussion in the campaign. As the number of reforms increased, voters were significantly more likely to argue that a heightened level of policy discussion occurred during the campaign.

THE LINK TO CITIZEN ENGAGEMENT AND SATISFACTION

Beyond ties to campaign assessments, it is important to determine whether campaign reform bears any relationship to citizen assessments of the political system. For a long time, the public has been disengaged and dissatisfied with government. Nearly half of the eligible electorate does not cast ballots, and many of those who do vote remain unhappy with the choices. Despite the rise of democracy in many parts of the world, Americans are dubious about the quality of their own elections.

In particular, we were interested in two measures of connectedness: engagement with the campaign process and satisfaction with the election result. The first item was measured through the following question:

Thinking just about the election for the U.S. House of Representatives in your district, how closely would you say you followed the contest? 1) very closely – I read newspaper accounts and followed the campaign regularly, 2) fairly closely – I watched it and generally followed what was happening, 3) Just somewhat closely – I saw the ads and a few news stories, but was not really interested, 4) not very closely – this race was not important to me, or 5) did not follow at all – only voted and did not do much else.

For our measure of voter satisfaction, we posed the following question:

Thinking about the election results for U.S. House of Representatives in your district, would you say you were pleased and satisfied with the outcome, displeased and dissatisfied with the outcome, or feel neutral and had no strong feeling one way or the other?

Responses were coded 1 for pleased, 2 for neutral, and 3 for displeased.

Both of these measures tell us important things about the public mood. For years, there has been concern over declining political participation and citizen disinterest in the electoral process. The engagement question relates directly to how people feel about the system and how closely they follow contemporary campaigns. The satisfaction question meanwhile taps a variety of sentiments, from whether they liked the winning candidate to whether their "bottom-line" feeling about the election was positive. It is an overall measure of how "pleased and satisfied" they were with the election outcome.

We undertook 10 different regressions (having formal debates, having issue forums, the presence of codes of conduct, pledges to avoid negative

Table 5-6. Regression Results for Campaign Reform Efforts on Voter Engagement

	Voter Engagement	Voter Engagement
Issue forums	.25 (.11)*	—
Summary campaign reform index	—	.10 (.05)*
Party identification	.08 (.07)	.15 (.08)
Ideology	−.15 (.08)	−.13 (.10)
Sex	−.03 (.11)	−.003 (.13)
Age	−.08 (.02)***	−.06 (.02)**
Income	−.001 (.03)	.03 (.04)
Education	−.02 (.03)	−.06 (.04)
Race	.06 (.15)	.09 (.18)
South/non-South	−.08 (.11)	−.14 (.14)
Constant	2.72 (.46)***	2.16 (.59)***
Adjusted R^2	.07	.05
F statistic	4.43***	2.50**
N	388	279

$*p < .05;\ **p < .01;\ ***p < .001.$
Note: The numbers are unstandardized regression coefficients, with standard errors in parentheses. The number of asterisks indicates the statistical significance of the coefficient.
Source: National Public Opinion Survey, 2002.

campaigning, and the summary campaign reform index for voter engagement and voter satisfaction with the election result). Eight of the 10 regressions produced no significant association between reform and either voter engagement or satisfaction. It didn't matter to these voter perceptions whether there were debates, codes of conduct, or pledges to avoid negativity.

The only two factors that showed significant relationships are included in Table 5-6. These were voter engagement and having issue forums and the overall campaign reform index. Districts where there were issue forums were more likely to have voters who felt engaged in the electoral process than places where there were no forums. Areas where voters had a chance to see candidates grappling with the issues and responding to citizen questions were linked to voters reporting that they followed the campaign more closely.

The same relationship was present for the overall campaign reform index. This scale was an additive index measuring the presence of each of the four reform features (debates, issue forums, conduct codes, and pledges to avoid negativity). Districts that rated highly on this index were more likely to have citizens who claimed they followed the congressional campaign in their area. This suggests that there was some payoff in citizen's eyes from organizations that were able to get candidates to participate in issue forums.

The failure of any of the other reform items to have an association with electoral outcome satisfaction is noteworthy because it shows the obstacles facing reformers interested in making voters feel better about the system. If the presence of reforms does not help to elevate how pleased and satisfied people are with the outcome of congressional races, it becomes even more difficult to increase their overall satisfaction with the political system. Obviously, there are many things that affect systemic satisfaction beyond individual election outcomes. This would include factors such as economic performance, foreign policy success, a sense that the country is moving in the right direction, and feelings about the trustworthiness and values of particular leaders. But voters who do not like the electoral result will be more difficult to persuade that things are moving in a positive manner.

CONCLUSION

In this chapter, we find that there was only a limited association between seeing campaign reform and various measures of campaign quality, such as positive tone, voter knowledge of candidates, and satisfaction with the electoral outcome. It did not matter whether there were debates, issue forums, conduct codes, or pledges to avoid negativity in congressional contests. Optimists' hopes that reform would elevate public thinking about the quality of electoral races were not borne out by this analysis.

In addition, there was no evidence that campaign reform was associated with more informed voters. Using a simple measure such as knowledge of the winning candidate's name, there was no proof that districts where some reforms took place generated greater voter information. Citizens in these areas were no more likely to know the name of the winning candidate or feel better about the campaign in general. This shows that reformers have a long path to follow before they will reach their ultimate goal of an informed electorate.

Nonetheless, there was a significant relationship between the presence of reform efforts in a voter's district and citizens believing there was more issue discussion during the campaign and reporting they were more engaged in the process. This demonstrates that campaign reform efforts have some effect on improving voter opinions toward electoral campaigns, but that it is limited and not consistently strong.

In the eyes of ordinary citizens from across the country, our findings demonstrate once again that reforms that are understandable and visible have the highest chance of success. They are easy to grasp and straightforward in their implementation. Voters know how to assess these events, and reporters devote considerable time reporting what happens in these venues.

From a citizen's perspective, issue forums are an ideal example of an effective reform. They generate considerable insight for voters and feature positive appeals from candidates. Since they generally allow citizens to pose questions directly to candidates outside of the filtering process undertaken by reporters, they are very popular with the public. Voters see them as authentic experiences that allow them to gauge aspects of a contender's background, character, and values. This gives forums the best shot of the reforms we have examined of reviving citizen confidence in the electoral process.

SIX

Improving the System

I n Jonathan Swift's imaginary country of Lilliput described in *Gulliver's Travels*, the Emperor chose new public officials by staging a "Dance on the Rope."[1] Political aspirants would jump on top of a rope, and whoever jumped the highest without falling off was awarded the new office. Although this criterion for electoral performance was arbitrary and bore little relationship to the duties of the office, it was a system that was open, clear, and egalitarian in the way it operated. Anyone could seek the office, and at the end of the "campaign," there were no disputes over who had won.

While democracies would not want to emulate this selection process, our contemporary system leaves a lot to be desired from the standpoint of democratic elections. Americans remain quite cynical about their political process and unhappy with the style and substance of campaigns for public office. Our empirical analysis shows there is little consistent evidence that proposed reforms have improved campaign discourse or conduct in the current period. Based on our findings, there is more support for the doubts of reform "skeptics" than that for the hopes of "optimists."

In this chapter, we step back from the details of our research and address three fundamental questions about campaign reform. Can the kinds of reforms that have been proposed recently have a positive effect? And, whether by those means or others, what is the likelihood that we will see system-wide change in the quality of information politicians provide when they campaign for reelection? Finally, are there other reforms that would make a significant difference in the way our electoral system operates?

IMPACT OF THE REFORMS THAT WERE ATTEMPTED

Our concern is with improving campaign discourse and campaign conduct, and ultimately the state of democracy itself. While many ideas have been put forth to improve the quality of American campaigns, we have been most concerned with the imposition of voluntary codes of conduct on candidates for office; the dissemination of "best practices" that were followed in winning campaigns, so that future campaigns could have models on which to draw; and self-regulation of conduct by the campaign consultant industry. During the 2002 midterm electoral cycle, various reform groups attempted to implement each of these ideas, some in specific districts, others throughout the nation.

We measure proposed changes by the extent to which competitive campaigns are seen to be substantive and civil as judged from three perspectives: the perceptions of consultants who worked in those campaigns (seen through our survey instrument, individual interviews, and focus groups), the views of voters about the contests, and independent assessments by academics on the ground in competitive districts who studied the content of news, ads, debates, direct mail, phone calls, and candidate Web sites. Because the ultimate goal of improving campaign discourse and conduct relates to actual behavior and conduct, we employ multiple approaches in order to get a complete picture of reform impact.

In doing this, we find a mixed record of achievement. Although some alterations, notably ones that are simple to implement and visible to citizens and reporters, have some associations with improved tone and substance, more complex reforms generally have been ineffective. There was little evidence that professional training schools, pledges to avoid negativity, or voluntary codes of conduct improved the electoral process. In most cases, voters did not perceive improved information flows or a style of campaigning that helped them hold leaders accountable at election time. As we argue in this chapter, these findings have important ramifications for the future of campaign reform and the way groups and advocates seek to improve the electoral process.

We now turn to more far-reaching questions: What is the likelihood that a code of conduct would be effective were it promulgated? What are the incentives and disincentives for consultants to follow such a code? What are the incentives and disincentives for candidates to implement best practices of campaign and debate conduct? What is the likelihood that the campaign consultant industry could effectively self-regulate?

These questions fall naturally into two parts. First, do the incentives outweigh the disincentives for candidates and consultants to adopt codes of campaign practices and to follow them if they were adopted? Second, can the campaign consultant industry follow the model of others, such as lawyers, doctors, or even fund-raisers for nonprofits, and self-regulate, either through entry via an accreditation procedure or through a tough, enforceable code of conduct? We will deal with these two facets separately.

INCENTIVES FOR CAMPAIGN DISCOURSE AND CONDUCT REFORM

From talking with, studying, and observing campaign professionals, it is not obvious that consultants have clear incentives to follow conduct codes, implement best practices of campaign and debate conduct, and self-regulate their industry. The strategy of reform through voluntary action – either signing and complying with voluntary codes of conduct, agreeing to eschew negative advertising, or searching out and adopting best practices – relies on candidates' and consultants' conclusions regarding their own self-interest. What the optimists hope to do is to convince candidates and their consultants that it is in their best interest, carefully thought through, to follow the reform agenda, because the campaigns will be more successful if the candidates and consultants do so.

When we discussed the potential for these kinds of reforms with the industry leaders we interviewed, we were struck by the uniformity of opinion that the decision whether or not to sign a code was a "strategic" decision, not a moral or ethical decision, and that the decision whether or not to comply was "tactical," not moral or ethical. Similar to the views of reform skeptics, they wanted to know whether the reform would help them win and would there be any negative fallout if they did not accept the reform. These conclusions seemed so obvious to the consultants that they required little or no discussion.

> I think in a handful of cases, discussions about no negative pledges came up and they were strategic decisions on, you know, if you're ahead, yeah, let's try and get the other guy to do it. But it was a strategic decision on whether to do that or not.

Once candidates have signed pledges, they do not like to break them, because they do not want to break their word. But, no one enforces the pledge. For example, the Institute for Global Ethics, the organization most closely associated with this reform effort, states clearly that they will not be "ethics police," and they are ill-equipped to play that role in any case. The media might play it, but they do not. Rather they trumpet the signing of pledges and might cover allegations that one candidate or another has gone negative, but they do not investigate the merits of those claims. So, again in the words of one of those whom we interviewed:

> I mean, just from a practical standpoint, you don't want to hamstring yourself. I mean, you don't want to make a big show of a pledge, I won't campaign negatively, but then you find yourself behind at the end of the campaign and it's the only way to come back.

Even some of those promulgating these reform efforts understood their limitations. Before we commenced this research project, we interviewed those most involved in advocating all of these reforms. We asked the advocates of both voluntary codes of conduct and of adopting best practices as seen in other campaigns how they thought campaigns would react, in a close race in the final days, if they had something negative about their opponent ready to go and felt that going negative at that time would make the difference. In every case, the response was that the campaign would go negative and that the kind of reform envisioned by codes or other exposure to best practices would not alter that situation.

The basic problem with the voluntary codes of conduct is that they misread candidate and consultant incentives. The biggest incentives for candidates are to win. Candidates do not run races in competitive elections in order to be thought of as good guys. They invest their lives, their time, and their egos in running to win. Consultants want to make money. And they make money if they are hired by campaigns. Campaigns hire consultants who have proven track records, consultants who win.

CNN's Judy Woodruff interviewed veteran political consultant Raymond Strother on his book, *How a Redneck Helped Invent Political Consultants:*

> Woodruff: It's pretty clear from your book that you don't think there are many scruples left in political consulting. For someone who looks at politics from the outside, what should they know about political consulting and what really makes it work?

> Strother: Win at any cost. You justify any action whatsoever for victory. In my business, you're never hired for a bad campaign, for a losing campaign. You're never hired if you lose by one vote.

You're only hired if you win. If you lose too many campaigns, you're out of business. You're on the street in this business. It's a tough, tough, tough business. So what you set up is a rivalry between political consultants and they influence candidates to do things that probably shouldn't be done in a campaign

And negative campaigning has been shown to be more effective than positive campaigning.[2] As another of our interviewees put it:

We had a candidate who had a very good record on women's issues, the Republican candidate. He spent fifteen hundred points over about three weeks telling people about how good he was, which was a position that was not typical for a Republican. Basically, after the fifteen hundred points nobody cared. Nobody paid attention to it.

He could not move his candidate's numbers in a positive direction by remaining positive. His conclusion was to go negative, not because he wanted to do so but because he felt he owed it to his candidate. His job was to give the candidate, in whom he believed and for whom he worked, the best chance of winning office. He followed the tactics he thought best – as the context of the campaign evolved, not in some theoretical sense – to succeed in that task.

Neither candidates nor consultants see it in their "enlightened self-interest" to adopt best practices that might lead to victory when other tactics are more likely to lead to victory. Consultants are conservative by nature, not politically conservative but professionally conservative. They do in the next campaign what has been successful in the last campaign. They will go negative as long as it is shown to win. They will stop going negative – if they think that is what is needed to win – when and only when they feel that going negative will hurt them more than it will help them.

When another strategy is proven successful over an extended period of time or when the strategy of going negative stops working in close races, the paradigm may shift. But occasional successes do not make a pattern. Pleas to improve the overall quality of the election process do not resonate with those who are concerned about winning elections and maintaining a business. It is important to understand these basic incentives.

As Richard Fenno pointed out years ago, there are major differences between individual and institutional incentives. He posed the apparent paradox through a wonderful title, "If, as Ralph Nader Says, Congress Is the Broken Branch, Why Do We Love Our Congressmen So Much?" Based on his analysis, Fenno argued that we love individual legislators because they talk themselves up while denigrating Congress as an institution and other members: "I'm not like those others. I'm your guy. I'm the guy you love."[3]

Similarly candidates – even those same Members of Congress as candidates – decry negative campaigning while they engage in it. One of the best strategies used in congressional midterms is to attack the opponent for negative campaigning. The strategy was successful in case after case, even if the opponent's campaign was not really negative. The point was made clearly. Attack the system; attack the other players; use surrogates if you can; but stay above the fray. The goal was not to improve the ways in which citizens view elected officials or even the institutions of government. The goal was to win a seat in one of those institutions.

Our conclusion on this point is that the system is not likely to be changed by these reforms. More than that, in an ironic way, some of the reforms contribute to the problem, because they give candidates another means of going negative, by accusing opponents of violating a pledge or of adopting unfair campaign tactics, whether the opponent is doing so or not.

THE POTENTIAL FOR INDUSTRY SELF-REGULATION

Just as candidates and consultants have no strong incentives to sign voluntary codes of campaign conduct,[4] consultants have no reason to sign ethics codes such as those promulgated by the American Association of Political Consultants (AAPC). The AAPC cannot become an effective self-regulating organization because there are no commonly accepted standards necessary to join the profession nor to remain in it. You rise in the profession by succeeding. You stay in it by continuing to succeed. While some subspecialties such as polling or fund-raising might have commonly accepted professional standards, general consulting does not. You cannot, therefore, have standards for accreditation.

What distinguishes political consulting from other "professions" that do successfully self-regulate? According to Eliot Freidson, "There are some kinds of expertise which are so valuable or potentially dangerous, or which are so complex and esoteric, that consumers are unable to choose competent practitioners without the aid of formal testimonials to competence and reliability."[5] The organizations of those with that level of expertise must self-regulate or give in to state regulation. Organizations that fit this description have a number of important characteristics. They are "centered on the body of knowledge and techniques...and on the training necessary to master such knowledge and skills."[6] And they have achieved a requisite level of prestige and autonomy.

This statement leads directly to another reason why the AAPC cannot become a self-regulating organization. Autonomy of a profession involves control over recruitment, training, and continued practice of a craft because of recognition that the skills and techniques are so specialized that only skilled practitioners can judge others. Put simply, political consulting does not cross this threshold.

Anyone can put himself or herself forth as a political consultant. If that person wins an election for candidate clients, particularly for underdog candidate clients, the reputation of the nascent consultant will be enhanced. And they will move forward from there. Candidates looking for consultants do not look for certificates from training schools or for credentials; they look for evidence of success. As two of consultants we interviewed put it:

> You know, frankly, the guys that get hired are the ones who are shown to win or have done it a lot. And so I don't know if all of, sort of attaching all of these sort of certifications and things of that... trying to put kind of the veneer of civilized conduct onto campaigns is going to change the basic problem.

Or

> Well, my one thing, in terms of presenting this as, okay, well I went through this campaign management school, I went through this ethics training and in presenting it to clients something that, I mean, this is sort of a tangential concern. ... And I think that adding some roster of a campaign ethics training program might not give that impression [of concern for the candidates' winning and local issues]. Might instead give a sort of, again, no disrespect, like a... impression that I think some candidates in some parts of the country might be, maybe not, you know, find unattractive, but not necessarily find attractive.

The skills needed to achieve success are more art than science. Whereas pollsters must know certain statistical methods to ply their craft effectively, consultants must have a feel for the electorate – and that cannot be measured or tested, except through practical experience. As consultants cannot control the training for or entry into their profession – all but required for self-regulating organizations according to all of the literature on the field we reviewed – it is difficult for them to police themselves.

Moreover – and this is a crucial point for the consulting industry to achieve some level of self-regulation on ethical standards – there is no agreement on the details of an ethical standard to apply to consultants' use of kinds of advertisements for their clients. Compare these two views of whether consultants should advise clients to use misleading ads:

> And if we're talking about honesty or candidness or whether that glass is half empty or half full, we're doing a disservice to the people who are having to make a choice between somebody who's in this squabble and somebody who's defining those terms. They should be talking about the issues that are important, not about whether or not that glass is half empty or half full.

Or

> Yeah, I have big problems with the word misleading. We like to believe we're just excellent at misleading attacks. . . . But we saw opportunities where we could make that a documentable distinction. But I guess if I were to sign this I'd feel a lot, have a lot more problems making those cases.

To illustrate this point further, during the course of our interviews with industry leaders, we presented the same scenario to eight different consultants. We described a situation that had actually occurred during the 2002 midterm election that we felt represented an egregious violation of commonly acceptable practices. We asked the interviewees to state their opinion of the advertisement run by the Democrats on behalf of Montana Senator Max Baucus in which they used a commercial ad run by his opponent nearly two decades earlier to criticize his business practices, but did so in such a way as to raise questions about his opponent's sexual orientation.

All eight consultants were familiar with the ad; it had achieved a level of fame (or notoriety, depending on one's view) in the profession and generated national media attention. Three found it to be totally unacceptable. Three thought it acceptable but foolish. The other two, including one who had worked for the candidate portrayed in the ad, found it both acceptable and effective. Those who felt it acceptable justified their opinion because the ad was true and did not distort the image portrayed by the candidate himself. Those who found it unacceptable objected to the implication of possible homosexuality in the ad, despite the fact that the opponent had produced the ad himself. If there is such disagreement among industry leaders on an example like this, what kinds of actions would lead to acknowledgment that acceptable standards had been violated?

Most consultants agree with the AAPC member who recalls signing their pledge: "I'm a member of that. I signed that pledge, but I think it's such a low standard, a low bar, it's pretty easy to achieve it." In this consultant's view, one signs it because one assumes that no one else actually is paying attention to it. There is very limited enforcement, even against those who do violate the pledge. And to emphasize the emptiness of this action, more than one of those interviewed volunteered that they were AAPC members but would resign rather than answering any charges brought against them. In the words of one consultant, "I have been a member of the AAPC for years, to help support the industry and give those coming along whatever advice I have. But in all my years no potential client – not one – has ever asked if I were a member. And frankly if they ever questioned my ethics, I'd be out of there in a New York minute."

To summarize, if one is looking for short-run or even intermediate-run changes in the electoral process, we do not see evidence that promotion of standards, best practices, or self-regulation by the consultant industry is likely to lead to the desired results. If one is satisfied with the view that the process might improve in the long run, these methods might make some sense. But we would add that the evidence on this front is not clear either. Changing the process requires consideration of the incentives that move those who are involved in the process. Winning and earning a reputation that can lead to business success are incentives far higher on the participants list than improving the process. Reforms that do not recognize these incentives are doomed to have limited impact.

PROSPECTS FOR SYSTEM-WIDE CHANGE

None of us is a skeptic by nature. Each of us believes that the electoral system in the United States could better serve our democratic values. But we are not sanguine about the likelihood of systemic change in how campaigns are run, not in the discourse that marks those campaigns, not in the conduct of the candidates and consultants, and not in their perceptions of what aspects of the campaign are in fact most important – those that can lead to victory. Based on our in-depth interviews, focus groups, and national surveys of voters and consultants, we do not believe there is much evidence in support of the likelihood of system-wide change in the campaign industry, arising through the promotion of standards, best practices, and industry self-regulation. That does not mean, however, that no improvement in the process is possible.

As we argued with our typology in Chapter 1, reforms that are clearly defined and understandable in the eyes of consultants and voters and address specific features of interest to the voters have the highest probability of success. Those are changes that are easy to understand, visible to all involved, and make it difficult for candidates to mislead the public. Debates and issue forums are examples of simple and easy reforms that generate a lot of voter information. They generally feature less negative rhetoric from the candidates and are very popular with the media and voters. They also are less likely than debates to degenerate into slugfests, replete with nasty one-liners.

In contrast, reforms such as pledges to avoid negative campaigning are not very effective with voters because they are too complex, not easy to grasp, and too easy for candidates to manipulate. For instance, there is no widely accepted definition of what constitutes negativity. One person's attack is another individual's piece of relevant information about a candidate's character or issue position. When one candidate "goes negative" in the middle of an election campaign, the other candidate typically responds in kind with the justification that "the other person started it." With this type of reform, then, candidates in competitive races are not motivated to stick to their pledge because, when the rhetoric becomes negative, it is too easy for each side to blame the other for the escalation and to continue to mislead voters about their opponent. There is no enforcement mechanism for individual candidates; and in any event, the lion's share of the most negative, misleading, and deceptive communications is produced by "third-party" organizations apart from candidate operations.

Based on similar reasoning, we do not think that any form of industry self-regulation is a strategy likely to find much success. Industry reforms occur far from the public view. They are out of sight and out of mind; and if they are out of the voter's mind, there is little incentive for consultants to worry about them. The consulting industry is unlike the medical and legal professions. In the campaign world, there are few barriers to entry. Professional associations with these characteristics tend to exert little power in terms of sanctioning members who engage in bad behavior. Although the AAPC may have some limited power through moral suasion over consultants, the association has not chosen to make much use of this authority and probably would not be very successful should it make such an attempt.

The most glaring obstacle to industry self-regulation is not just the lack of a professional standard for the consulting industry but rather the lack of agreed-upon ethical standards among consultants. There is considerable disagreement among consultants regarding what is and what is not an acceptable campaign practice. For instance, while some consultants find comparative advertising, contrasting candidate qualifications and issue stances with those of opponents, acceptable, others view this as negative advertising or at least the first step on a slippery slope to negative advertising. Although consultants may not be able to define negative advertising, per se, they know it when they see it. The question is, however, what do they see? One person's blatantly negative, out-of-bounds ad is another's masterpiece.

Moving beyond the endemic problem of a lack of agreed-upon standards, how would industry principles be enforced and by whom? Would candidates care if a consultant were sanctioned by an oversight organization such as the AAPC if said consultant had a 90 percent win rate? In an industry where winning often is the sole benchmark of excellence, the prospect that candidates would no longer hire such a consultant is highly suspect. Indeed, we find it hard to believe that candidates would not hire consultants merely because some in the industry found their campaign practices unprofessional. As stated above by several consultants, one person's unethical activity is another's perfectly legitimate campaign strategy. Therefore, this strategy seems to be doomed to failure.

Some reformers have argued that requiring consultants to attend campaign schools that explicitly discuss ethical considerations in campaigning should have the result of improving the quality of campaign discourse. They view this – or even more radical moves toward credentialing – as another way to increase the professionalism of the consulting industry.

In our consultant survey, we asked if the respondent had attended such a school. In contrast to the expectations of reformers, attendance at a campaign school appears to have a generally negative impact on the impressions that campaign consultants had of the election (Table 6-1). For instance, graduates of campaign schools were 11 percent more likely than nongraduates to argue that the overall tone of the election was more negative than in previous years. Similarly, they also were more likely

Table 6-1. Consultant Impressions of Campaign By Consultant
Attendance at Campaign School

	Attended	Did Not Attend
Overall tone more negative	49 (39)	38 (33)
Tone in own campaign negative	64 (51)	58 (51)
Less issue discussion	43 (34)	22 (19)
Campaign ads helped voters	44 (35)	58 (51)
Pledge not improve campaign behavior	40 (32)	55 (48)

Values represent percentages; N for subcategory is in parentheses.
Source: Campaign Consultant Survey, 2002.

(64 to 58 percent) than their brethren to believe that the tone in their race was more negative than in previous races on which they have worked. Additionally, they were 21 percent more likely than those who had not attended a campaign school to believe that there was less issue discussion than in previous electoral cycles, as well as 14 percent less likely than their counterparts to believe that campaign ads in their race had not helped voters to better distinguish between candidate qualifications and issue positions.

How can one explain these findings that are so contrary to what reformers anticipated when they proposed improved consultant training? Graduates of campaign schools have been involved in long and thoughtful discussion of what constitutes ethical campaigning and what does not. Moreover, they have become deeply familiar with the intellectual debate over negative campaigning. We argue that, as a consequence of their schooling, they are more sensitive to and aware of any efforts by an opposition campaign to smear their clients and even those of others in their own campaigns to use techniques that they find objectionable. Thus, they may be more likely to view issue comparisons as negative smear tactics and less likely to see the pointing out of issue differences between candidates as a discussion of the issues.

Further supporting this proposition, campaign school graduates were 15 percent less likely than nongraduates to argue that pledges to run an ethical campaign do not improve campaign behavior. This finding is consistent with the aforementioned argument about the uniqueness in graduates' viewpoints, as those who have attended campaign schools are more likely to view efforts to improve campaign behavior as having an impact on campaigning. Nothing in the data we have gathered supports the argument that consultants who attended a campaign training school ran different races than did those who did not. In the final analysis, their success or failure is measured in the same way as is that of any political consultant, by whether or not their candidates won, not by the level of professional training they had acquired.

Although organizations such as the AAPC have devoted resources to and worked with several universities to set up campaign training schools, they have not been able to get around one of the basic problems that confronts any reform in this area: There are no agreed-upon standards; what one program considers to be pushing the ethical envelope, another program might view as perfectly acceptable.

Furthermore, it appears that staff campaign school attendance may actually have a negative effect on raising the level of substantive campaign discourse. Keeping in mind that the data presented above are measuring consultant impressions of a midterm campaign, it still is somewhat alarming to learn that campaign school attendance by staffers or candidates appears to result in less issue discussion during campaigns. This finding may be the result of the method of training employed at campaign schools. They want to produce successful consultants; ethical considerations are important to them, but not primary. Their curricula typically place more emphasis on learning how to activate a candidate's base and drive a wedge in the opponent's base, rather than on how to engender a meaningful dialogue with voters about the leading issues in the campaign. But this emphasis is a reflection of the incentives that drive the profession; the goal is not to engender meaningful dialogue but rather is to win elections. To that end, with even worse consequences for those who seek to enhance substantive campaigning, graduates may be well versed in how to avoid issue discussions that might damage their candidate's chance of electoral success. Schools have very different goals from those of campaign reformers. In general, they want to make better consultants, that is, those with the knowledge to help their candidates win elections, not to improve the performance of democratic political systems.

Additionally, one must remember that the immediate goal of someone entering a campaign school is to find a job in the industry. Many consultants who have worked in the industry for decades argue that such campaign school attendance is a waste of time, believing that the only way to learn about the campaign process is from the "school of hard-knocks." Of course, the directors of the campaign schools disagree. However, resistance among older, established consultants, many of whom head successful consulting firms, further undermines the ability of the schools and the industry to reach agreed-upon accreditation or credentialing standards.

Do these schools hold any promise for reform of campaign discourse and campaign conduct? If they do, their potential for impact is in the long run, not the short. And here the scenario might be somewhat more positive. If more and more consultants come through these schools and remain in the profession, and if the graduates of these schools do think seriously about the ethical dilemmas they will face, and if they do think about them with conceptual, philosophical tools that are removed from the day-to-day strategic and tactical concerns of campaigning, when this new generation rises to positions of professional leadership, their overall view might well be different from that which is prevalent today. But there was a great deal of conditionality in that scenario – and even if all the conditions are met, we are envisioning a long-run marginal change, because nothing the campaign schools do can alter the basic incentive system at work.

We found one more piece of disconcerting evidence for the likelihood of any system-wide change. That concerned a requirement imposed as a result of McCain–Feingold campaign finance legislation requiring candidates personally to appear in and say they approved television and radio advertisements financed by their campaign committees. The idea behind this proposal was to stem the tide of attack ads. If one personally appears in and takes responsibility for advertising appeals, the hope was that there would be fewer attacks and more civil discourse.

Yet evidence from the 2004 presidential nominating campaign provides at best ambiguous support for this reasoning. That contest featured a large number of attack ads that were approved by the candidate. Having personally to say you were responsible for the advertisement appeared to act as little or no constraint on the level of negativity by these candidates. Other candidates, most notably Senators Kerry and Edwards, ran more positive ads. In the general election, the pattern seems mixed – with the Bush–Cheney campaign running a large number of negative ads right from the start while the Democratic ticket relied more heavily on surrogates to attack the president, the vice president, and their records.

In the same vein, agreeing to avoid negative campaigning and abide by a code of conduct can be thought of as proxy variables for self-regulation by those working on the campaigns. When candidates agree not to use attack ads, they are self-regulating their campaigns and consultants. Similarly, when they pledge to conduct their campaigns according to agreed-upon rules, they are agreeing to self-regulate.

According to our voter survey results, however, the pledge to avoid negative campaigning had no significant effect on improving campaign tone, elevating issue discussion, or increasing voter turnout. These represent measures of better campaigns in the eyes of reformers, but agreeing to a code of conduct had little effect on campaign conduct.

As we have already noted, in the current campaign environment, many candidates rely on surrogates to do the negative campaigning. We have seen clear evidence of this trend in recent elections, at times with surrogates campaigning despite efforts by the candidates to have them refrain from doing so.

In Texas, incumbent Democrat Martin Frost and incumbent Republican Pete Sessions were placed in the same district, as part of a Republican effort to gain seats in the House. Frost and Sessions agreed to denounce negative advertising and any commercials funded by any groups other than the two candidates. The only problem was that the National Republican Congressional Committee did not agree with Sessions's pledge and continued to run ads aimed at Frost.

> What this means, in the end, is that a clean-campaign pledge may have no practical effect at all. Candidates may sign official-looking documents when agreeing to such pledges, but they are not binding in any fashion. Outside interests are not required to abide by them and, in many cases, have no desire to do [so].[7]

While candidates might be willing to sign pledges themselves, the activities of others in the electoral process result in a situation in which the overall tone of the campaign and level of campaign discourse fail to meet the standards of those trying to elevate campaigns.

Improving campaigns through media oversight appears to be an ineffectual means of reform. At first blush, media oversight may seem like an excellent way to effect campaign reform. Reporters from various media outlets could review campaign commercials, check facts, and report their findings to the public. However, politics is full of gray areas. What constitutes a "fact" often is disputable. Few news outlets are willing to commit the time and resources to pursue this type of agenda in any case. Thus, reliance on media oversight to reform campaigning would be somewhat problematic as evidenced by the dissatisfaction shown even in areas in which the media attempt to perform this function.

Each of the widely advocated campaign reforms, then, has serious drawbacks. Our inability to find strong, consistent, and enduring effects from specific campaign reform activities thus leads us to conclude that the current reform agenda has not succeeded in achieving its objectives. While there are some areas that look encouraging, such as the tie between issue forums and improvements in issue discussion, the prospects for system-wide change do not look very promising.

THE FUTURE OF REFORM

Lest we appear overly pessimistic about campaign reform, there are some measures we feel do have a better chance of improving the electoral process. Our assumption is that strengthening the conduct of campaigns and the quality of the discourse can happen only if the basic incentives that drive candidates and campaign consultants are addressed. To do so, one must recognize that the driving force in both cases is winning elections. Reform efforts that try to change perceptions of self-interest will not change the incentives.

The question for reformers is not how to change practice, but rather how to change the incentives. In our view, the target of reformers should not be the candidates and the consultants. The target for reform should be the voters. Citizens can speak and penalize bad behavior and unfair tactics. Perhaps the most promising recent experience was in the Iowa caucuses, the first step in the Democratic nominating process in 2004. The campaign was shrill, with the leading contenders – former Vermont Governor Howard Dean and Congressman Richard Gephardt of Missouri – perhaps the most negative in their rhetoric. And the Iowa Democratic voters rejected them both, opting instead for the two senators in the race, John Kerry and John Edwards, each of whom put forth a more positive message. That lesson from the Iowa voters was not lost on the other candidates. Their campaign rhetoric came down several notches, not because they were forced to do so, but because they had seen what was working – in that particular political context.

The larger question for reformers is how to make citizens expect or even demand more information, civil campaigns, and substantive debate. That is no easy task, but those intent on improving the American system of governance have never shrunk from difficult assignments. In the twentieth century, men were convinced that it was right to give women the franchise, even though it was controversial, because society demanded it. In the same respect, civil and voting rights for African-Americans, which once were thought impossible, were enacted through decades of work by ardent reformers. And in terms of party reform, leaders were made to cede power to the rank and file because they were convinced that doing so was in their best interest.

In the case of campaign reform, the injustice is less visible and more difficult to depict. It is challenging to show that all citizens are losing because of the ways in which campaigns are run. It is difficult to document the tax on society from attack ads, unfair tactics, and vague appeals. Yet we all can see the toll that has been taken on our system in the form of low voter turnout, high public cynicism, and contentious campaigns.

Only by convincing citizens that our system can and should do better will we be able to alter the incentives facing campaigners. When candidates lose because of voter backlash against nasty or misleading advertisements, political professionals will take note and adjust their strategies. Actions that affect the probability of winning or losing are taken very seriously by candidates and their consultants.

Elections are central to democratic processes, and reform organizations need to continue working on changes. All of the consultants we talked to and all the individuals who hold leadership position in major civic organizations believe it is important to continue to seek to improve our electoral process. At a time when many countries around the world are turning to democracy and looking to the United States for guidance on how to develop democratic institutions, it is worthwhile to continue to emphasize campaign reform. The problems of unethical and uncivil discourse are not going to disappear any time soon. Since these and other examples of campaign behavior continue to make many citizens cynical about the democratic process in this country, it is important to gain a better understanding of this important area. As one of those we interviewed put it:

> I think the absence of [reform efforts] like that would be a damn shame. Not that I believe they actually have an immediate impact. But I think that the longer these kinds of programs are around the more of a bottom up effect they'll have. And hopefully if you get enough competent, qualified, ethical, certified people who by the way can win, because ultimately that's what it comes down to. But I'd rather have somebody who's going to win and who's certified and competent and ethical than somebody who's going to win who isn't.

While our research clearly shows the limits of some approaches to campaign reform, it also is apparent that other activities have produced discernible effects and are likely to have a positive impact on our electoral system. Though we are not very sanguine about the likely success of every current reform proposal, we believe there are several ideas that meet the criteria of improving elections and strengthening the quality of campaign discourse.

In particular, we are optimistic about reforms that are in the tradition of changing the way in which the current process functions – one involving detailed and well-publicized nonpartisan critiques of highly visible campaigns; the second, an increased emphasis on debates and issue forums; and the third, a call for programs to educate political journalists to cover campaigns in a way that focuses citizen attention on issues and important related matters. In addition, if one were to look for more radical change that could alter the electoral process in more fundamental ways, we raise an approach that if implemented would alter the paradigm for running an effective campaign by broadening the audience at which campaigns are aimed.

Because of the combative nature of American campaigns, one reform that comes out of our research emphasizes detailed and nonpartisan critiques of candidates in highly visible campaigns. Elections are inherently conflictual. Candidates, parties, and groups compete to present themselves in the most favorable light. They take positions and engage in strategies designed to make themselves look good. To the extent that taking positions makes them come across well, they will be quite specific on the issues. And if campaigning negatively or in a misleading manner causes them to look bad in the eyes of the electorate, the disincentives from taking such action will be strong.

Consultants understand that political communication involves a considerable degree of give and take. Nonpartisan groups have credibility with voters and the media that makes them very important messengers. One reform we are suggesting would have nonpartisan groups monitor a small number of highly visible elections very closely and publicize widely the practices in those campaigns that do not meet the highest standards. These groups can educate the public about the shortcomings of the process and about the use of misleading appeals or scare tactics that discourage some citizens from voting and thus play a very destructive role. They can bring attention to abusive practices, and they can force campaigners to justify specific claims and campaign styles.

As one consultant put it, "If Pew and similar organizations weren't doing what they're doing, I think it would just be a lot worse out there." This individual used the analogy of a stop sign to compliment nonpartisan reform groups. "If you have a stop sign at an intersection, you don't, you know, you can't quantify how many accidents it stops," the person said. But one suspects that some accidents were prevented.

To date the efforts to monitor campaigns result in criticism of some campaign tactics, but not in widespread publicity of that criticism. If criticism is below the radar screen of the largely inattentive public, it is not nearly so effective an incentive to avoid tactics that were subject to criticism as it could be if the criticism were given as much play as the offending ads themselves. The efforts so far have been like stop signs for a number of campaigns. What we are suggesting is big, bold red lights for a smaller number of highly visible campaigns – with the implied threat that any campaign was subject to similar scrutiny. Such an effort would be difficult; to be credible there could be no appearance of bias – and the sponsoring reform organization would be vulnerable to attack for partisan campaigning. But the rewards might well be worth the risks. For this kind of effort could quickly alert the public to the difference between the kinds of campaigns to which it has been exposed and those which could improve the process as a whole.

Another effort that we would encourage is to promote mechanisms such as debates and issue forums that provide substantive information to voters. These types of forums have been very promising, and efforts to promote them would help to improve the electoral process. But these efforts must also address the structural problems inherent in communicating to the public when many campaigns are going on in the same media market at the same time. Merely having issue forums or debates is not sufficient, if no one sees or hears them. Improving debates is a worthwhile goal only when combined with increased efforts to disseminate them.

We feel that programs that educate journalists how to improve their campaign coverage and get citizens to pay closer attention to issues and important related matters are very valuable. Voters need help at election time, and the media are among the most crucial intermediary players in the election process. Programs that train journalists to develop new skills and styles of coverage that inform the public contribute to the strategic environment in which consultants operate. Several consultants told us that reforms with the highest probability of success were those that involved the media. If criticism about campaign tactics is in the media, both candidates and consultants pay close attention to it.

One consultant we talked with stressed the importance of press training, advocating "training the press to cover campaigns beyond just the process of it, which they like to cover, [and] who's ahead in money or polling." Getting journalists to adopt "a broader perspective of coverage of issues and candidates," perhaps by appealing to their sense of duty to the public, would be very valuable, according to our focus group participants.

Another consultant wanted journalists to take a pledge to pay attention to politics, especially on the television side of the media. "They're the ones who really provide information to voters . . . and they rarely cover political races." This sentiment was echoed by a consultant who said that if he could wave a magic wand and alter something about the process, the change would involve the media. "I'd like to have the news media pay closer attention to campaigns," he said.

Journalists already devote some attention to advertising through ad watches, but consultants believe there also should be a "phone watch" and an "Internet watch" that would monitor campaign tactics in these areas. In some ways, consultants believe, journalists are not very knowledgeable about the political process. "Journalists, number one, are incredibly naive about politics and don't ask the right questions, don't understand what makes a good or bad ad, what makes an ad accurate or inaccurate." Improving their training and coverage – especially that for local papers – would make a substantial contribution to the quality of the electoral process.

In making this recommendation, we are fully aware of limitations inherent in the structure of the news media. Media cannot cover all campaigns equally, especially in major markets in which literally dozens of campaigns are run simultaneously. But they can improve on what they are doing; and they can concentrate enough efforts so that campaigners and consultants would fear negative coverage if they overstepped certain ethical standards. And that deterrence would be a major step forward in improving campaign discourse.

Although these reforms will improve campaign conduct in certain ways, we believe it will take much bigger thinking out of the conventional box and more radical change to make an enduring difference. Toward that end, we believe it is worthwhile to consider the implications of further spread of the expanded period for voting now used in some states and some form of universal suffrage for American elections.

Since campaigners generally do whatever it takes to win, the most substantial reform suggestion that came out of our focus group research is one that would completely change the nature of the electorate and, in the process, alter the incentives candidates and consultants have to engage in bad behavior.

Right now, American presidential elections typically attract the participation of half of the eligible electorate, while off-year congressional contests feature voter turnout of around one-third of those eligible to cast ballots. State and local races sometimes feature turnout as low as 10–15 percent of eligible voters.

In this situation, candidates have incentives to engage in a number of hurtful practices. They can play to their base in extreme ways and ignore the preferences of more moderate voters. They can attempt to drive down the turnout of those supporting the opposition candidate while raising the participation of those who support them. They can use negative and misleading advertisements to manipulate the preferences of those who decide at the last minute. They don't worry much about their role in promoting a sense of system legitimacy among the general public.

We think there are two structural reforms that would alter the incentives campaigners have to engage in these practices. The first one takes advantage of recent laws in many states that encourage people to cast absentee or mail ballots well before Election Day. In some states, between 25 and 40 percent of the electorate are casting ballots in the month leading up to the election. In a campaign where voters are casting ballots over the course of a month and with candidates not knowing exactly when citizens are voting, it becomes much harder to target negative, misleading, and inaccurate appeals at the end of the campaign, when journalists don't have time to cover the barrage and opponents don't have an opportunity to reply.

Expanding the political contest from a single day to the month before the election shifts campaign dynamics in a way that discourages turnout suppression and unfair campaigning and encourages more even-handed campaigning on the part of candidates. These reforms are still relatively new, and little systematic research has gone into the consequences that follow from them, other than increased turnout. Such a research effort should be encouraged, particularly examining how the different systems employed in different states have similar or different effects.

The second change would be even more radical, involving compulsory voting laws. Twenty-nine countries around the world have enacted some form of legislation (either statutes or constitutional provisions) that requires citizens to exercise their civic responsibility of participating in some levels of elections. These include Argentina, Australia, Belgium (the first one to introduce this in 1892), Bolivia, Brazil, Chile, Costa Rica, Cyprus, Dominican Republic, Ecuador, Egypt, Fiji, Gabon, Greece,

Guatemala, Honduras, Italy, Liechtenstein, Luxembourg, Mexico, Nauru, Paraguay, Peru, Philippines, Singapore, Switzerland, Thailand, Turkey, and Uruguay.

In some countries, citizens are required to cast ballots only if they are registered to vote, which limits universal voting to those who are registered. In other places, voting is required of all who meet basic eligibility requirements, such as being citizens aged 18 years or older. The rigor of the sanction for not voting varies widely. Typically, universal voting laws make voting a civic obligation with a token civil fine of $5–$30 for infractions. Those with a legitimate reason for not voting (such as hospitalization, serious illness, or incarceration) are exempted from enforcement.

Not surprisingly, turnout in these countries generally is quite high. Countries such as Belgium, Australia, and Luxembourg, which have strict enforcement, feature turnout that is around 90 percent or higher. For example, recent parliamentary elections in Belgium generated a turnout of 91 percent, while races in Luxembourg attracted 89 percent and in Australia, 95 percent voted. Other nations with looser enforcement had turnouts that ranged from 70 to 80 percent.

From the standpoint of improving campaign conduct and discourse, universal voting offers promise by reducing incentives for unhealthy campaign practices, increasing incentives to appeal to moderate rather than extreme voters, and promoting a greater sense of system legitimacy. Turnout suppression strategies using negative campaigning would be useless under such a system. Candidates would be encouraged to appeal to a broader range of constituents through civil rhetoric, not just the "base" vote within each party that currently responds to highly partisan appeals. Higher turnout would force campaigners to use campaign tactics that improve, not undermine, the basic legitimacy of the system. By imagining structural changes that alter campaign incentives in fundamental ways, we feel that campaign reform can be very successful and can improve the tenor of campaigns and the quality of electoral discourse in the United States.

While some observers might see universal voting laws in the United States as politically unfeasible, we should note that America has a long tradition of experimenting with many different kinds of election rules at the state and local level. Efforts to introduce universal voting rules in selected cities and states would offer greater hope of implementation (plus a laboratory in which to assess whether this reform would improve the election process) than if undertaken just at the national level.

Another approach that would move our system closer to universal suffrage would be to register each citizen automatically after his or her eighteenth birthday, a reform that could easily be implemented because of technological advances in recent years. Experience in states with less restrictive voter registration laws shows that the need to register is often the largest deterrent keeping a citizen from voting. Removing that deterrent would bring more of the public to the polls. Research that explored the possibilities of these kinds of reforms would broaden the discussion of how to improve American elections in a much more fundamental way than typically has occurred.

We present these recommendations not because we necessarily believe them feasible, but because we think that they are based on a theoretical foundation that has the potential to meet the goals of reformers. In undertaking this research, we were struck both by the difficulty in achieving positive results and the worthy desire of all involved to improve American democracy. While we are not sanguine about the ability of some of the current efforts to reach their goals, we believe those efforts have been worthwhile, at the least in pushing participants to think about the consequences of their actions. And we believe that reform organizations are right to emphasize the importance of finding keys to success in this area. In the long run, we believe that with proper attention to electoral incentives, campaign reform can make a positive difference in improving the nature of campaign discourse and conduct in the United States.

APPENDIX A

Data and Methodology

This research relied on several different data sources to investigate the quality of campaign discourse in the congressional elections – and the impact of reform efforts on that discourse. In July 2001, we identified House and Senate seats deemed likely to be competitive in November 2002. Our goal was to study competitive districts because these are the districts most likely to see the kinds of problems identified in the past and because competitive races are those most important in determining the overall outcome of an election. We identified the seats drawing on the expertise of three independent analysts who report on congressional elections – Rhodes Cook, editor of the Rhodes Cook Letter; Stuart Rothenberg, editor of the Rothenberg Political Report; and Amy Walter, House of Representatives editor of the Cook Political Report. We also relied on the judgment of experts on our Peer Review Panel and our Advisory Board to confirm our original choice of districts, amending the list according to their suggestions (see Preface).

We contacted scholars who lived or worked in or near the districts and states we had identified to serve as our consultants in these districts. By relying on the academics who knew the local terrain, we brought to bear detailed expertise in these competitive races. Our original list included 20 House seats and 5 Senate seats. We added two additional House seats 2 months into the data-gathering phase of this research because of increased interest in these races. The final list thus included 22 U.S. House districts (Arizona 1, Colorado 7, Connecticut 2 and 5, Florida 22, Illinois 19, Indiana 2, Kansas 3, Maryland 8, Maine 2, Minnesota 2, Mississippi 3, North Carolina 8, New Hampshire 1, New Mexico 2, Nevada 3, Ohio 3 and 17, Pennsylvania 17, Texas 23, Utah 2, and Washington 2) and 5 U.S. Senate races (Maine, Minnesota, North Carolina, New Hampshire, and Texas).

In consultation with the scholars serving as consultants, the Advisory Board, and the Peer Review Panel, we devised separate protocols to monitor advertising, news coverage (separate samples of days and weekly summaries), debates, and Web sites. These protocols were tested before the data-gathering began. Coder reliability was found to be within allowable limits during the pretest period. These detailed protocols are available from the authors on request.

Content analysis of campaign discourse was carried out from August 2002 through the November election. Consultants submitted interim reports throughout the campaign season, and we were able to monitor data collection to assure consistency across campaigns, to the extent possible. Each consultant also submitted a summary evaluation of the campaign he or she monitored, affording us another opportunity to assess comparability.

We have data sets that include observations of 1,263 examples of campaign literature, 522 individual newspaper stories and 100 individual television newscasts, 639 weekly summaries of media news, 52 candidates' Web sites (with multiple observations of most), and 39 candidate debates. These five data sets provide evidence for most of our conclusions about the content of campaign discourse and the effectiveness of reform efforts on the 2002 electoral process. These data sets will be made available to the broader research community for secondary analysis once our project is complete.

Immediately after the campaign's completion, we undertook a national telephone public opinion survey of 642 registered voters, 70 percent of whom said they had voted in the 2002 midterm elections. This survey was undertaken from November 8 to 11, 2002, and had a margin of error of plus or minus four percentage points. The poll was supervised by the authors and completed by the offices of Peter Hart and Robert Teeter, a bipartisan team of prominent national pollsters. The sample was compiled through random digit dialing and was designed to be geographically representative of the entire country.

The goal of the survey was to examine voter awareness and evaluation of various reform ideas. For example, the survey studied the extent to which voters were aware of a variety of campaign reforms, such as debates, issue forums, voluntary codes of conduct, and whether candidates in their congressional district or Senate race pledged to avoid negative campaigning. This allowed us to see if there were differences in voter assessments of campaign tone, civility, and substance, based on whether debates and forums had taken place in their area and whether districts where candidates signed pledges to avoid negative campaigning were related to larger views about the campaign. The survey questions are listed in Appendix B.

We also contracted with Peter Hart and Bob Teeter to collaborate on a telephone survey of consultants active in the 2002 congressional campaigns in competitive districts. We compiled the list of districts, expanding on those selected above as the campaign evolved. We also produced the list of consultants working in those campaigns and, working with Hart and Teeter, devised the survey instrument. That survey instrument appears in Appendix C.

The consultant survey was conducted between November 6 and November 25, 2002, right after the conclusion of the election. We successfully contacted 197 consultants. The group was quite representative of the total population we had identified, with a number of consultants who worked in open seats, for incumbents, and for challengers, in House races, and in Senate races. The sample did include more Democrats than Republicans, but the disparity was small enough that we could still look at interparty differences. Through this survey we looked at how consultants viewed the races in which they were involved during the elections. Among the topics investigated in this survey were opinions about the tone and conduct of the races and whether their individual races relied on formal debates, issue forums, voluntary codes of conduct, pledges to avoid negative campaigning, or had staff who attended campaign training schools. We looked at awareness and evaluations of campaign reform efforts, as well as whether races that had one or more of the reform activities demonstrated any difference in tone or campaign conduct.

In addition, we interviewed 18 industry leaders from across the country – 10 in person and 8 on the telephone. These interviews, some of which are quoted in this book, allowed us to further explore some of the conclusions that we drew from the survey of consultants and to seek the opinion of these individuals on the implications of those conclusions for the future of reforms in this area.

Toward the same ends, we contracted with Peter Hart to run two focus groups with leading campaign professionals. The first one was held on April 14, 2003, with 8 consultants who reside in Washington, DC. Five of these were Democrats and 3 were Republicans. The group included a cross-section of different types of consultants, ranging from pollsters and media consultants to direct mail specialists, fund-raisers, and general strategists. The second discussion took place on April 24, 2003, with 10 consultants who lived outside of Washington, DC. It included

5 Democrats and 5 Republicans with an equally diverse range of sub-specialties within the consulting industry. Geographically the group spanned the nation – two were from the West Coast, one from Denver, one Dallas, one Chicago, one Columbus, one South Florida, one Atlanta, and two from New England.

This research effort was designed to probe in greater depth how consultants felt about campaign reform and what kinds of changes would improve the nature of American elections. We asked a number of different questions, such as their view of the consulting industry, their familiarity with and evaluation of campaign reform efforts, impressions of Election 2002, and suggestions they had for improving campaign discourse in the United States. The protocols used for the focus groups are found in Appendix D.

Each of these efforts was undertaken to evaluate the content of campaign discourse in the midterm congressional elections and the visibility, viability, and effectiveness of various campaign reform efforts. By relying on multiple data collection, we sought to gain both breadth and depth of knowledge about how the most competitive elections were contested. In particular, we looked at voter and consultant evaluations of campaign discourse and awareness of reform activities, their evaluation of these reform efforts, and an analysis of whether reform initiatives showed any relationship to public trust, perceptions about campaign civility and substance, and overall views about the political system. Through the study of data from a variety of sources, we are able to discuss the impact of campaign reform on campaign conduct and whether elections can be made better at promoting the ability of voters to judge candidates for legislative office in the United States.

Public Opinion Survey

QP1 As you know, on November fifth there was an election for U.S. Congress and other offices. Many people were not able to vote. How about you – were you able to vote in person on Tuesday, had you already voted by mail or absentee ballot, or didn't you get a chance to vote?

Yes, voted in person 1
Yes, voted by mail/absentee ballot 2
No, did not vote 3
Not sure 4

I'd like to ask you a few questions about Tuesday's election. For these remaining questions, please focus on the election for federal offices, such as U.S. Congress, and not on state or local races, such as those for governor in certain states or for state legislature.

QP2a Thinking just about the election for the U.S. House of Representatives in your district, how closely would you say you followed the contest? (READ LIST. ACCEPT ONLY ONE RESPONSE.)

Very closely – I read newspaper accounts and followed the
    campaign regularly 1
Fairly closely – I watched it and generally followed what
    was happening 2
Just somewhat closely – I saw the ads and a few news stories,
    but was not really interested 3
Not very closely – this race was not important to me 4
Did not follow at all – only voted and did not do much else 5
Not sure 6

QP2b Thinking about the election results for U.S. House of Representatives in your district, would you say you were pleased and satisfied with the outcome, displeased and dissatisfied with the outcome, or feel neutral and had no strong feeling one way or the other?

Pleased and satisfied 1
Displeased and dissatisfied 2
Neutral and no strong feeling 3
Not sure 4

QP2c Thinking honestly, do you happen to know the name of the winning candidate for the U.S. House of Representatives in your Congressional district? (IF "YES," ASK:) And what was the candidate's name?

Yes, and know name of candidate 1
Yes, but do not know the name of candidate 2
No, do not know who won 3
Not sure 4

QP2d Now I'd like to mention several factors that some people think about when they are deciding how to vote. For each factor that I mention, please tell me how informed you feel you were about that particular part of the campaign for U.S. Congress – very informed, fairly informed, just somewhat informed, or not very informed.

The candidates' backgrounds and qualifications
The candidates' records and issue positions
National policy issues
Local policy issues

Very informed 1
Fairly informed 2
Just somewhat informed 3
Not very informed 4
Not sure 5

QP2e Do you feel the campaign ads which ran in your district were generally helpful and added to your ability to understand the positions and qualifications of the two candidates and helped the election process, or do you feel that the ads were not helpful and were just aimed at providing negative information about the opponent and hurt the election process?

Helped 1
Hurt 2
Some of both (VOL) 3
Not sure 4

QP3a Now I'm going to read you some things that happened in some Congressional elections around the country. For each one, please tell me to the best of your knowledge, whether that happened in your Congressional district.

Televised debates in which both major candidates participated
Issue forums in which both major candidates appeared
A pledge by the candidates to abide by a specific code of conduct in running their campaigns
A pledge by the candidates to avoid negative
Attack-oriented campaign strategies

Yes, happened in district 1
No, did not happen in district 2
Not sure 3

QP3b Now I'd like to ask you specifically about one of these things – pledges by candidates to abide by a specific code of conduct in running their campaigns. Would you say that these pledges are very important, fairly important, just somewhat important, or not very important?

Very important 1
Fairly important 2
Just somewhat important 3
Not very important 4
Not sure 5

IF QP3a = No, did not happen in district OR QP3a = Not sure

THEN GO TO: QP4

(ASK ONLY OF RESPONDENTS WHO SAY THAT THERE WAS A PLEDGE BY THE CANDIDATES TO ABIDE BY A CODE OF CONDUCT IN QP3a.)

QP3c And based on what you saw and heard how well did the candidate or candidates live up to their pledge to abide by a specific code of conduct in running their campaigns – very well, fairly well, just somewhat well, or not very well?

Very well 1
Fairly well 2
Just somewhat well 3
Not very well 4
Not sure 5

(ASK EVERYONE.)

QP4 Thinking about the campaigns that were run by the candidates for U.S. House of Representatives in your district this year, how would you describe the overall tone of those campaigns – highly negative, somewhat negative, equally positive and negative, somewhat positive, or highly positive?

Highly negative 1
Somewhat negative 2
Equally positive and negative 3
Somewhat positive 4
Highly positive 5
Not sure 6

QP5 Compared to past elections, do you think that this year's election campaign was generally more positive, about the same, or more negative?

More positive 1
About the same 2
More negative 3
Not sure 4

QP6 Compared to past elections, would you say that there was more discussion about policy issues in this campaign or less discussion about policy issues?

More discussion of issues 1
Less discussion of issues 2

About the same discussion of issues (VOL) 3

Not sure 4

QP7a In this year's election for federal offices, such as U.S. Congress, a national nonpartisan organization called the Institute for Global Ethics supported by the PEW Charitable Trusts asked candidates to sign a voluntary code of conduct or pledge to run their campaigns with high ethical standards and to refrain from negative, attack-oriented campaign strategies. Before I just mentioned it, had you heard of this effort to get candidates to sign a code of conduct in their campaigns?

Yes, had heard of effort 1

No, had not heard of effort 2

Not sure 3

QP7b And from what I just read, do you think that encouraging candidates to sign such a voluntary code of conduct or pledge would be very effective, fairly effective, just somewhat effective, or not very effective in improving campaign behavior and the way campaigns are run?

Very effective 1

Fairly effective 2

Just somewhat effective 3

Not very effective 4

Not sure 5

FACTUALS: Now I am going to ask you a few questions for statistical purposes only.

PartyID Regardless of how you may be registered, how would you describe your overall point of view in terms of the political parties? Would you say you are mostly Democratic, leaning Democratic, completely independent, leaning Republican, or mostly Republican?

Mostly Democratic 1

Leaning Democratic 2

Completely independent 3

Leaning Republican 4

Mostly Republican 5

Not sure 6

Ideolog Thinking about your general approach to issues, do you consider yourself to be liberal, moderate, or conservative?

Liberal 1
Moderate 2
Conservative 3
Not sure 4

Those are all the questions I have for you. Thank you for your time and cooperation.

Consultant Survey

WIN–LOSE (DO NOT ASK.) Record whether campaign won or lost.

Won 1
Lost 2

RACETYP Record RACE type (from call sheet).

1–Democratic Senate incumbent 1
2–Democratic Senate challenger 2
3–Democratic Senate open seat 3
4–Republican Senate incumbent 4
5–Republican Senate challenger 5
6–Republican Senate open seat 6
7–Democratic House incumbent 7
8–Democratic House challenger 8
9–Democratic open seat 9
10–Republican House incumbent 0
11–Republican House challenger 1
12–Republican open seat 2

STATE STATE (from call sheet).

DISTRIC RECORD CONGRESSIONAL DISTRICT (from call sheet).

. . . .
Numeric Range. . . . .
Don't Know. . . . .

I'm calling from the offices of Peter Hart and Robert Teeter, the poll-sters who do the NBC/*Wall Street Journal* Survey. We have been asked to conduct a nationwide bipartisan study among high-level campaign strategists. We would really appreciate your taking a few minutes to answer some questions for this very important project about the 2002 campaign. The project is being done for research purposes only and we absolutely guarantee that individual responses will be kept completely confidential. This will take no more than twelve minutes, and is only being conducted among a select group of campaign professionals.

Gender (DO NOT ASK.) Record respondent's gender.

Male 1
Female 2

(ASK ONLY OF TYPES 2, 3, AND 4.)

Q1a How many campaigns have you personally been involved in or worked on in the past ten years? (IF "NOT SURE," RECORD "DK.")

. . . .
Numeric Range. . . . .
Don't Know. . . . .

(ASK ONLY OF TYPES 1, 5, 6, 7, AND 8.)

Q1b In how many campaigns were you personally involved in the 2002 GENERAL election cycle? (IF "NOT SURE," RECORD "DK.")

. . . .
Numeric Range. . . . .
Don't Know. . . . .

All the questions I ask you in this survey will pertain to the race you worked on this election cycle.

(ASK EVERYONE.)

Q1c How would you compare this particular race to others you may have worked on in the past few years – was it extremely interesting, very interesting, pretty interesting, about average, or not very interesting?

```
Extremely interesting............................................1
Very interesting.................................................2
Pretty interesting ..............................................3
About average....................................................4
Not very interesting.............................................5
Not sure ........................................................6
```

Q1d And again thinking about this race compared with others you may have worked on in the past few years, was this campaign very well-funded, pretty well-funded, just somewhat well-funded, or not very well-funded?

```
Very well-funded ................................................1
Pretty well-funded ..............................................2
Just somewhat well-funded .......................................3
Not very well-funded.............................................4
Not sure ........................................................5
```

Q2a Thinking for a moment about the 2002 general election cycle overall, not just this race, do you think that this year's campaign was generally more positive, generally more negative, or had about the same tone as recent election cycles?

```
Generally more positive .........................................1
Generally more negative..........................................2
About the same tone as recent cycles ............................3
Not sure ........................................................4
```

Q2b And again, thinking about the 2002 general election cycle overall, would you say that there was more discussion of policy issues this year, less discussion of issues this year, or about the same amount of discussion as in past election cycles?

```
More discussion .................................................1
Less discussion .................................................2
About the same amount of discussion..............................3
Not sure ........................................................4
```

Q3 Please tell me whether the following activities or events were part of or applied to the campaign you worked on.

Formal debates in which both major candidates participated
Issue forums in which both major candidates appeared
A pledge by either or both candidates to abide by a specific code of conduct in running their campaigns
A pledge by either or both candidates to avoid negative campaigning
Staff or candidate attendance at a campaign training school

Yes, applied/was a part of the campaign 1
No, did not apply/was not part of the campaign 2
Not sure 3

Q4a Now I'd like to ask you a few questions about ads in the campaign that you were working on. In answering these next few questions, please think only about the ads that related to or were in support of your candidate, not your opponent. Thinking about ALL the television and radio ads that related to your candidate's campaign, about what share was paid for by the candidate's actual campaign committees – more than three-quarters, between one-half and three-quarters, between one-quarter and one-half, or less than one-quarter?

More than three-quarters 1
Between one-half and three-quarters 2
Between one-quarter and one-half 3
Less than one-quarter 4
Not sure 5

Q4b And, again, thinking about those ads that related to or were in support of your candidate, about what share was paid for by national or state political parties – more than three-quarters, between one-half and three-quarters, between one-quarter and one-half, or less than one-quarter?

More than three-quarters 1
Between one-half and three-quarters 2
Between one-quarter and one-half 3
Less than one-quarter 4
Not sure 5

Q4c And about what share of the ads that related to or were in support of your candidate or were designed to defeat your opponent were paid for by third-party interest or issue advocacy groups? (READ LIST IF NECESSARY.)

More than three-quarters 1
Between one-half and three-quarters 2
Between one-quarter and one-half 3
Less than one-quarter 4
Not sure 5

Q4d I'd like to talk now about the ads run by your opponent's campaign, that is, the ads paid for by the official campaign committee of your opponent, and not by outside, independent groups. I'm going to ask you what percentage of the total ads run were primarily designed as positive ads for your opponent, what percentage were primarily designed as negative ads against your candidate, and what percentage were primarily designed as ads comparing the two candidates. Please keep in mind that the total of the three percentages should add to 100 percent. (MAKE SURE RESPONDENT UNDERSTANDSQUESTION. IF "NOT SURE" RECORD AS "DK.")

Primarily designed as positive ads for your opponent
Primarily designed as negative ads against your candidate
Primarily designed as ads comparing the two candidates
What percentage of the total ads run were . . . ?

. . . .
Numeric Range. . . . .
Don't Know. . . . .

Q4e Now thinking about the ads run by independent groups not associated directly with your opponent's campaign, but supportive of his or her campaign or designed to defeat your candidate, I'd like you to tell me what percentage you think were primarily designed as positive ads for your opponent, what percentage were primarily designed as negative ads against your candidate, and what percentage were primarily designed as ads comparing the two candidates. Again, the total of the three percentages should add to 100 percent. (MAKE SURE RESPONDENT UNDERSTANDS QUESTION. IF "NOT SURE" RECORD AS "DK.")

Primarily designed as positive ads for your opponent
Primarily designed as negative ads against your candidate
Primarily designed as ads comparing the two candidates
What percentage of the total ads run were . . . ?

. . . .
Numeric Range. . . . .
Don't Know. . . . .

Q4f Do you feel that the campaign ads that ran in your race were generally helpful, added to voters' ability to understand the positions and qualifications of the two candidates, and helped the election process, or do you feel that the ads were not helpful, were just aimed at providing negative information about the opponent, and hurt the election process?

Helpful 1
Hurt 2
Some of both (VOL) 3
Not sure 4

Q5a Compared with the last mid-term election in 1998, did the voter turnout percentage in your race go down, stay about the same, or go up?

Turnout went down 1
Turnout stayed the same 2
Turnout went up 3
Not sure 4

Q5b Thinking about this race in the context of other races you may have worked on this cycle or in recent years, would you describe the overall tone of this race as highly negative, somewhat negative, equally positive and negative, somewhat positive, or highly positive?

Highly negative 1
Somewhat negative 2

Equally positive and negative 3
Somewhat positive 4
Highly positive 5
Not sure 6

Q6a During the campaign, a national nonpartisan organization called the Institute for Global Ethics supported by the PEW Charitable Trusts asked candidates for federal office to sign a voluntary code of conduct or pledge to run their campaigns with high ethical standards and to refrain from negative, attack-oriented campaign strategies. Before I just mentioned it, had you heard of this effort to get candidates to sign this code of conduct in their campaigns?

Yes, had heard of effort 1
No, had not heard of effort 2
. . . . (Skip to Q6d)
Not sure 3
. . . . (Skip to Q6d)

(ASK ONLY OF RESPONDENTS WHO SAY THEY HAVE HEARD OF THE EFFORT IN Q6a.)

Q6b1 Did your candidate take this particular pledge or agree to this voluntary code of conduct?

Yes, candidate took pledge/agreed 1
No, candidate did not take pledge/agreed 2
Not sure 3

(ASK ONLY OF RESPONDENTS WHO SAY THEY HAVE HEARD OF THE EFFORT IN Q6a.)

Q6b2 Do you happen to know whether your opponent took this particular pledge or agreed to this voluntary code of conduct?

Yes, opponent took pledge/agreed 1
No, opponent did not take pledge/agreed 2
Not sure 3

IF Q6b1 = No, candidate did not take pledge/agreed OR Q6b1 = Not sure

THEN GO TO Q6c2

(ASK ONLY OF RESPONDENTS WHO SAY THEIR CANDIDATE TOOK THE PLEDGE IN Q6b1.)

Q6c1 What was the main reason why your candidate took the pledge or agreed to the voluntary code of conduct?

....
....

(ASK ONLY OF RESPONDENTS WHO DO NOT SAY THEIR CANDIDATE TOOK THE PLEDGE IN Q6b1.)

Q6c2 What was the main reason why your candidate did not take the pledge or agree to the voluntary code of conduct?

....
....

(ASK ONLY OF RESPONDENTS WHO DO NOT SAY THEY HAVE HEARD OF THE EFFORT IN Q6a.)

Q6d If your candidate had been asked to take such a pledge or agree to a voluntary code of conduct, do you think that he or she would have been more likely to agree or more likely to refuse?

More likely to agree 1
. . . . (Skip to Q7a)
More likely to refuse 2
. . . . (Skip to Q7a)
Depends (VOL) 3
. . . . (Skip to Q7a)
Not sure 4
. . . . (Skip to Q7a)

(ASK ONLY OF RESPONDENTS WHO SAY THEIR CANDIDATE TOOK THE PLEDGE IN Q6b1.)

Q6e Thinking honestly, how well would you say that your candidate and the campaign lived up to this pledge – very well, fairly well, just somewhat well, or not very well?

```
Very well . . . . . . . . . . . . . . . . . . . . . . . . . . . . . . . . . . . . . . . . . . . . . . . . . . . . . 1
Fairly well . . . . . . . . . . . . . . . . . . . . . . . . . . . . . . . . . . . . . . . . . . . . . . . . . . . . 2
Just somewhat well . . . . . . . . . . . . . . . . . . . . . . . . . . . . . . . . . . . . . . . . . . . . . 3
Not very well . . . . . . . . . . . . . . . . . . . . . . . . . . . . . . . . . . . . . . . . . . . . . . . . . . 4
Not sure . . . . . . . . . . . . . . . . . . . . . . . . . . . . . . . . . . . . . . . . . . . . . . . . . . . . . . 5
```

(ASK ONLY OF RESPONDENTS WHO SAY THEIR CANDIDATE TOOK THE PLEDGE IN Q6b1.)

Q6f And how much of an effect would you say that this pledge had on the overall tone of the campaign – a very big effect, a fairly big effect, just somewhat of an effect, or not much of an effect?

```
Very big effect . . . . . . . . . . . . . . . . . . . . . . . . . . . . . . . . . . . . . . . . . . . . . . . . 1
Fairly big effect . . . . . . . . . . . . . . . . . . . . . . . . . . . . . . . . . . . . . . . . . . . . . . . . 2
Just somewhat of an effect . . . . . . . . . . . . . . . . . . . . . . . . . . . . . . . . . . . . . . . 3
Not much of an effect . . . . . . . . . . . . . . . . . . . . . . . . . . . . . . . . . . . . . . . . . . . 4
Not sure . . . . . . . . . . . . . . . . . . . . . . . . . . . . . . . . . . . . . . . . . . . . . . . . . . . . . . 5
```

(ASK EVERYONE.)

Q7a The code of conduct put forth by the Institute for Global Ethics supported by the PEW Charitable Trusts calls on candidates in the course of their campaigns to engage in practices that strengthen public confidence in political campaigns overall. Specifically, the pledge includes a promise not to appeal to voters based on racism, sexism, religious intolerance, or other unlawful forms of discrimination, to refrain from false or misleading attacks on opponents, to document criticisms of an opponent's record, and to be honest and candid in dealing with the news media. From the description that I just read to you, do you think that encouraging candidates to sign such a voluntary code of conduct or pledge would be very effective, fairly effective, just somewhat effective, or not very effective in improving campaign behavior and the way campaigns are run?

```
Very effective . . . . . . . . . . . . . . . . . . . . . . . . . . . . . . . . . . . . . . . . . . . . . . . . . 1
Fairly effective . . . . . . . . . . . . . . . . . . . . . . . . . . . . . . . . . . . . . . . . . . . . . . . . . 2
```

Just somewhat effective 3
Not very effective 4
Not sure 5

Q7b Why do you feel that way? In what way would a voluntary code of conduct or pledge to refrain from negative, attack-oriented campaign strategies be effective in improving campaign behavior and the way campaigns are run?

And in what way would this code of conduct or pledge be less effective?

. . . .
. . . .

Q7c Are you a member of the American Association of Political Consultants?

Yes, member of American Association of Political Consultants 1
No, not a member of American Association of Political Consultants . . 2
Not sure 3

Q7d As you may know, the American Association of Political Consultants has a code of ethics. How familiar are you with this code – very familiar, fairly familiar, just somewhat familiar, not very familiar, or have you not heard of this before?

Very familiar 1
Fairly familiar 2
Just somewhat familiar 3
Not very familiar 4
Have not heard of it 5
. . . . (Skip to Q8a)
Not sure 6
. . . . (Skip to Q8a)

(ASK ONLY OF RESPONDENTS WHO SAY THEY ARE AT LEAST SOMEWHAT FAMILIAR WITH AAPC CODE OF ETHICS IN Q7d.)

Q7e Thinking honestly, do you think of this code of ethics more as a serious and important pledge or more as a formality that does not have much practical application?

Serious and important 1
A formality 2
Not sure 3

(ASK ONLY OF RESPONDENTS WHO SAY THEY ARE AT LEAST SOME-WHAT FAMILIAR WITH AAPC CODE OF ETHICS IN Q7d.)

Q7f How much of an effect do you think this code has on the behavior of your peers – a great deal, a fair amount, just some, not very much, or none at all?

A great deal 1
A fair amount 2
Just some effective 3
Not very much 4
None at all 5
Not sure 6

(ASK ONLY OF RESPONDENTS WHO SAY THEY ARE AT LEAST SOME-WHAT FAMILIAR WITH AAPC CODE OF ETHICS IN Q7d.)

Q7g And how much of an effect do you think this code has on your own behavior – a great deal, a fair amount, just some, not very much, or none at all?

A great deal 1
A fair amount 2
Just some 3
Not very much 4
None at all 5
Not sure 6

(ASK EVERYONE.)

Q8a Do you think that a professional organization such as the American Association of Political Consultants should be able to censure those who violate a code of ethics for campaign professionals?

Yes, should be able to censure 1
No, should not be able to censure 2
Not sure 3

Q8b The American Association of Political Consultants is considering developing a certificate training program for campaign professionals that would emphasize high standards in campaign practices. How useful do you think such a program would be to campaign professionals such as yourself – very useful, fairly useful, just somewhat useful, or not very useful?

Very useful 1
Fairly useful 2
Just somewhat useful 3
Not very useful 4
Not sure 5

Q9 Finally, how much of an effect do you think ad watches – that is, press coverage focusing on the accuracy of political ads – have had in making campaigns more careful about the content of their ads – a great deal of effect, a fair amount of effect, just some effect, not much effect, or no effect at all?

A great deal of effect 1
A fair amount of effect 2
Just some effect 3
Not much effect 4
No effect at all 5
Not sure 6

FACTUALS: Now I'm going to ask you a few questions for statistical purposes only.

QF1 How old are you?

18–24 1
25–34 2
35–44 3
45–54 4
55–64 5
65 and over 6
Not sure 7

QF2 Are you from a Hispanic or Spanish-speaking background? (IF "NO," ASK:) What is your race – white, black, Asian, or something else?

Hispanic 1
White 2
Black 3
Asian 4
Other 5
Not sure/refused 6

QF3 Generally speaking, do you think of yourself as a Democrat, a Republican, an independent, or something else?

Democrat 1
Republican 2
Independent 3
Other 4
Not sure/nothing 5

ZIP And may I please have your ZIP code?

. . . .
Numeric Range. . . . .
Don't Know. . . . .

Those are all the questions I have for you. Thank you for your time and cooperation.

APPENDIX D

Focus Group Protocol

INTRODUCTION

First, let's take a minute to go around the table and introduce ourselves. I'm sure many of you know each other, but give us your pseudonym and tell us a little bit about your work with campaigns in the past few years. I'm most interested in the kind of campaign work you do, not in which campaigns you've worked on.

Tell me how 2002 was different from other campaign years? What made it different in terms of tactics and techniques that you used?

1. What makes the business of campaigns difficult? Why is it different from other competitive professions?
2. What are some of the biggest challenges you've faced lately in campaigns?
3. In what ways has campaigning changed in the past five years? How about the past 10 years?

Thinking about the races you worked on in 2000 and 2002, how would you compare those races to races you worked on in previous years? Were they more interesting? In what ways?

WHAT IS YOUR STANDARD OF JUDGMENT IF THIS IS A GOOD CAMPAIGN OR A BAD CAMPAIGN? How do you decide beyond winning – what makes you feel good about your work in a campaign?

CAMPAIGN ACTIVITIES

I'd like to talk a little bit about some things that may have been part of campaigns you worked on in 2000 or 2002. I'm going to list some activities

that your campaign may have participated in during the campaign.
SHOW OF HANDS

Formal debates or issue forums – did your candidate participate in any
forum debates or issue forums in 2000 or 2002?
Why or why not?
What were the benefits of these debates or forums? In what ways
did they help the campaign? In what ways did they help the
voter?
What were the drawbacks? Did they affect the campaign in any
negative ways? What about voters?
*Taking a pledge to abide by a specific code of conduct in the campaign
or a pledge to avoid negative campaigning* – did your candidate take
either of these kinds of pledges?
Why or why not?
In what ways, if any, was this pledge beneficial?
In what ways, if any, was this pledge harmful?
A campaign school – did your candidate or anyone on the campaign
staff attend a campaign school or a campaign training program?
Why or why not?
In what ways, if any, was the school helpful?
In what ways, if any, was the school not helpful?

CAMPAIGN TONE

Thinking about the 2002 general election cycle overall, do you think last
year's campaign was generally more positive, generally more negative, or
had about the same tone as recent election cycles?
What kinds of factors contributed to the cycle being more positive?
What kinds of factors contributed to the cycle being more negative?
How do you think:
If you put yourself in the place of voters, do you think your answer
would be the same? How do you think voters would characterize the
2002 election cycle? Why?
What kinds of things do you think would stand out as positive?
What kinds of things do you think would stand out as negative?
In what ways do you think campaigns would have to change for voters
to feel they are positive?
**What do you think determines if a campaign is negative? How would
I know if a campaign is negative – what is the definition?**

Where do you see a negative campaign – ads, direct mail, speeches, debates or where?

How does one decide when it makes sense to go negative?

Has there ever been a year where you did not feel a negative campaign was necessary?

CAMPAIGN ADVERTISING

I'd like you to think for a moment about the ads run by your candidates in 2002. Would you say that the ads were mostly positive, mostly negative, or mostly neutral?

What kinds of factors in a campaign lead to decisions to run negative ads?

What kinds of factors in a campaign lead to decisions to run positive ads?

Do you feel that the campaign ads which ran in your race were generally helpful and added to voter's ability to understand the positions and qualifications of your candidate?

In what ways were the ads helpful for voters in making decisions?

In what ways were the ads helpful in helping and motivating voters to participate in the elections?

If you were to take all of the ads run by your campaign in 2002, what percent would you say were positive, and added to voters' ability to understand your candidate, and what percent were negative, and aimed at providing negative information about your opponent?

How do you think that affects voters' perception of your candidate?

How do you think that affects voters' perception of elections in general?

CAMPAIGN DISCOURSE

Thinking again about the election cycle overall, would you say there was more discussion of policy issues in 2002, less discussion about policy issues, or about the same amount of policy discussion? Why do you feel that way?

What factors in 2002 encouraged policy discussion within the campaign? Among voters?

What factors inhibited policy discussion within the campaign? Among voters?

In your opinion, do you think voters had enough information about the policy positions of your candidate to make informed choices in the election? Why do you feel that way?

Do you think voters would agree?

What kinds of information do you think voters need to make good decisions?

In what ways, if any, do you think the campaigns of 2002 failed voters?

What are the best ways for campaigns to communicate policy information and positions to voters?

What are the best ways for campaigns to encourage discussion between candidates and voters? How about among voters?

CODES OF CONDUCT AND ETHICS

As you may know, during the 2002 campaign a national nonpartisan organization called the Institute for Global Ethics supported by the PEW Charitable Trusts asked candidates to sign a voluntary pledge to run their campaigns with high ethical standards and to refrain from negative, attack-oriented campaigning. Before just now, had you heard about this effort?

Did any of your candidates happen to take this pledge?

What were the main reasons your candidate decided to take the pledge?

What were the main reasons your candidate decided not to take the pledge?

Do you happen to know whether any of your opponents took the pledge?

Thinking honestly, how well would you say that your candidate and the campaign lived up to the pledge?

Whether or not your candidate took the pledge, how much of an effect would you say that such a pledge would have on a campaign?

In what ways would it change a campaign for the better?

In what ways would it make the campaign better for voters?

In what ways would it make a campaign more challenging to run?

In what ways do you think that such a pledge could be effective in improving the ways campaigns are run and voters are informed? Are there ways that such a pledge would be ineffective in improving the way campaigns are run and voters are informed?

How many of you are members of the American Association of Political Consultants? How many of you know about the American

Association of Political Consultants code of ethics? What can you tell me about it?

Again, honestly, do you think of this code of ethics as a serious pledge, or as more of a formality?

How much of an effect do you think this code of ethics has on the behavior of your peers and on campaigns? In what ways does it have an effect?

Do you think that professional associations like the American Association of Political Consultants should be able to censure those who violate their code of ethics? Why or why not? What does that mean to you?

The American Association of Political Consultants is considering developing a certificate training program for campaign professionals that would emphasize high standards in campaign practices. How useful do you think such a program would be? In what ways would it be useful? In what ways would it not make a difference in the way campaigns are run and voters are informed?

One more thing before I let you go. When you are working on a campaign, how much do you think about ad watches? By ad watches, I mean press coverage focusing on the accuracy of political ads.

How effective do you think ad watches are in making campaigns more careful about the content of their ads?

Do you think ad watches have improved campaigns or helped voters? In what ways?

Notes

CHAPTER ONE: CAMPAIGN REFORMERS: OPTIMISTS, SKEPTICS,
AND REJECTIONISTS

1. Bruce Buchanan, *Renewing Presidential Politics*, Lanham, MD: Rowman & Littlefield, 1996; and *Presidential Campaign Quality: Incentives and Reform*, Upper Saddle River, NJ: Pearson/Prentice Hall, 2004.
2. Thomas Mann, "Linking Knowledge and Action: Political Science and Campaign Finance Reform," *Perspectives on Politics*, vol. 1 (March 2003), pp. 69–84.
3. V. O. Key, *The Responsible Electorate*, Cambridge, MA: Harvard University Press, 1966; and Morris Fiorina, *Retrospective Voting in American National Elections*, New Haven, CT: Yale University Press, 1981.
4. Samuel Popkin, *The Reasoning Voter*, Chicago: University of Chicago Press, 1991.
5. Richard Nadeau and Michael Lewis-Beck, "National Economic Voting in U.S. Presidential Elections," *Journal of Politics*, vol. 63, no. 1 (February 2001), pp. 159–181; and John Zaller, "Information, Values, and Opinion," *American Political Science Review*, vol. 85, no. 4 (December 1991), pp. 1215–1237; see also the classic work, Edward E. Tufte, "Determinants of the Outcomes on Midterm Congressional Elections," *American Political Science Review*, vol. 69, no. 1 (March 1975), p. 312, and works that have followed it, including James Campbell, "The Revised Theory of Surge and Decline," *American Journal of Political Science*, vol. 31, no. 4 (November 1987), pp. 965–979; Campbell, *The Presidential Pulse of Congressional Elections*, Lexington, KY: University of Kentucky Press, 1997; and Alan Abramowitz, *Voice of the People: Elections and Voting in the United States*, New York: McGraw-Hill, 2004.
6. Bruce Buchanan, *Presidential Campaign Quality: Incentives and Reform*, Upper Saddle River, NJ: Pearson/Prentice Hall, 2004; and Dennis Thompson, *Just Elections: Creating a Fair Electoral Process in the United States*, Chicago: University of Chicago Press, 2002.
7. Ken Goldstein and Paul Freedman, "Measuring Media Exposure and the Effects of Negative Campaign Advertising," *American Journal of Political Science*, vol. 43, no. 4 (October 1999), pp. 1189–1208; and Kenneth Goldstein, *Interest Groups, Lobbying, and Participation in America*, New York: Cambridge University Press, 1999.
8. Kathleen Hall Jamieson, *Dirty Politics: Deception, Distraction, and Democracy*, New York: Oxford University Press, 1992; L. Sandy Maisel, Cherie Maestas, and Walter J.

Stone, "Quality Challengers to Congressional Incumbents: Can Better Candidates Be Found?" in Paul S. Herrnson, ed., *Hardball Politics*, Upper Saddle River, NJ: Prentice Hall, 2001, pp. 12–40; L. Sandy Maisel and Walter J. Stone, "Determinants of Candidate Emergence in U.S. House Elections: An Exploratory Study," *Legislative Studies Quarterly*, vol. XXII (February 1997), pp. 79–96; and Roderick Hart, *Campaign Talk: Why Elections Are Good for Us*, Princeton: Princeton University Press, 2000.

9. Institute for Global Ethics national survey, December 15, 1999.

10. Pew Research Center national survey, November 10–12, 2000, with 1,113 registered voters. Survey archived at the Roper Center for Public Opinion Research POLL service.

11. Thomas Patterson, *Out of Order*, New York: Alfred A. Knopf, 1993; and Darrell M. West, *The Rise and Fall of the Media Establishment*, Boston: Bedford/St. Martin's Press, 2001.

12. Darrell M. West, *The Rise and Fall of the Media Establishment*, pp. 104–105.

13. Many of these efforts have been funded by major foundations including the Pew Charitable Trusts, the Carnegie Corporation of New York, the Smith Richardson Foundation, and the Ford Foundation.

14. Institute for Global Ethics national survey, "Poll Shows Voters Want Greater Civility, Ethical Behavior in Campaigns," press release, December 15, 1999.

15. Larry Sabato and Glenn Simpson, *Dirty Little Secrets: The Persistence of Corruption in American Politics*, New York: Times Books, 1996; and Larry Sabato, *Feeding Frenzy: How Attack Journalism Has Transformed American Politics*, New York: Free Press, 1991.

16. John Hibbing and Elizabeth Theiss-Morse, *Congress as Public Enemy: Public Attitudes Toward American Political Institutions*, New York: Cambridge University Press, 1995; and Larry Bartels and Lynn Vavreck, eds., *Campaign Reform*, Ann Arbor, MI: University of Michigan Press, 2000.

17. Bruce Cain, "Excerpts from Declaration of Bruce Cain in Badham v. Eu," *PS*, vol. 18, no. 3 (Summer 1985), pp. 561–567.

18. Daron Shaw, "Is Reform Really Necessary? A Closer Look at News Media Coverage, Candidate Events, and Presidential Votes," in Larry Bartels and Lynn Vavreck, eds., *Campaign Reform*.

19. Samuel Popkin, *The Reasoning Voter*, p. 8.

20. George Edwards, *Why the Electoral College Is Bad for America*, New Haven, CT: Yale University Press, 2004.

21. Steven Schier, *You Call This an Election?: America's Peculiar Democracy*, Washington, DC: Georgetown University Press, 2003; Stephen Wayne, ed., *Is This Any Way to Run a Democratic Government?*, Washington, DC: Georgetown University Press, 2004; and Anthony Corrado, Thomas E. Mann, Daniel R. Ortiz, and Trevor Potter, *The New Campaign Finance Sourcebook*, Washington, DC: Brookings Institution Press, 2005.

22. Thomas Patterson, *The Vanishing Voter: Public Involvement in an Age of Uncertainty*, New York: Alfred A. Knopf, 2002.

23. Ann Crigler, Marion Just, and Edward McCaffery, eds., *Rethinking the Vote: The Politics and Prospects of American Election Reform*, New York: Oxford University Press, 2004.

24. Although we were evaluating the overall impact of a series of grants funded by the Pew Charitable Trusts in the general area of campaign discourse, the foundation put no restrictions on our research. The Pew Charitable Trusts provided ample time and financial resources to collect data, analyze the campaign, and interpret the results. Indeed, in a personal meeting with Pew President Rebecca Rimel at the beginning of the research project, we were told to undertake an honest appraisal of campaign discourse, even if it meant concluding that the Pew Charitable Trusts had not succeeded in achieving its objectives of improving the conduct of American political campaigns.

25. Steven Schier, *You Call This an Election?*; Stephen J. Wayne, *Is This Any Way to Run a Democratic Election?* second edition, Boston: Houghton Mifflin, 2003; Ann Crigler, Marion Just, and Edward McCaffery, eds., *Rethinking the Vote*, New York: Oxford University Press, 2004; and Thomas E. Mann and Bruce Cain, *Party Lines: Competition, Partisanship, and Congressional Redistricting*, Washington, DC: Brookings Institution Press, 2005.

26. Stephen Ansolabehere and Shanto Iyengar, *Going Negative: How Political Advertisements Shrink and Polarize the Electorate*, New York: Free Press, 1995; Steven Finkel and John Geer, "A Spot Check: Casting Doubt on the Demobilizing Effect of Attack Advertising," *American Journal of Political Science*, vol. 42, no. 2 (April 1998), pp. 573–595; Ken Goldstein and Paul Freedman, "Measuring Media Exposure and the Effects of Negative Campaign Advertising," *American Journal of Political Science*, vol. 43, no. 4 (October 1999), pp. 1189–1208; Kim Kahn and Patrick Kenney, "Do Negative Campaigns Mobilize or Suppress Turnout?" *American Political Science Review*, vol. 93, no. 4 (December 1999), pp. 877–889; and Richard Lau and Gerald Pomper, *Negative Campaigning: An Analysis of U.S. Senate Elections*, Lanham, MD: Rowman & Littlefield, 2004.

27. Richard F. Fenno, Jr., *Home Style*, Boston: Little, Brown, 1978.

28. John Hibbing and Elizabeth Theiss-Morse, *Congress as Public Enemy*.

Chapter Two: Dissemination of Campaign Practices

1. Arthur Miller and Michael MacKuen, "Learning About the Candidates: The 1976 Presidential Debates," *Public Opinion Quarterly*, vol. 43, no. 3 (Autumn 1979), p. 344.

2. We enlisted the advice of Stu Rothenberg of the *Rothenberg Political Report*, Amy Walter of the *Cook Political Report*, and Rhodes Cook of the *Rhodes Cook Report* to arrive at a list of districts likely to be competitive, seven months before the election was held. Our eventual list included districts identified by at least two of these experts on congressional campaigns.

3. Amy Keller, "AU Survey Underscores Split Among Political Strategists," *Roll Call*, March 13, 2003, p. 1.

4. Annenberg Public Policy Center, University of Pennsylvania, "Stand By Your Ad: A Conference on Issue Advocacy Advertising," September 16, 1997, Washington, DC.

5. Magali Sarfatti Larson, *The Rise of Professionalism*, Berkeley, CA: University of California Press, 1977.

6. The AAPC has many members who are not active in campaigns; students in graduate programs, for instance. Similarly, many active in campaigns are not professional

political consultants but rather individuals who work on one or two campaigns and then go on to something else; they tend not to join the association.

7. Richard Morin, "Republican Strategist Luntz Censured by Pollsters for '94 Campaign Survey," *Washington Post*, April 27, 1997, p. A13.

8. Shawn Legendre, "Self-Regulating Organizations and the Professional Market," unpublished paper, July 30, 2002.

9. Darrell M. West, *Air Wars: Television Advertising in Election Campaigns, 1952–2004*, fourth edition, Washington, DC: Congressional Quarterly Press, 2005.

10. The survey methodology is discussed in greater detail in Appendix A.

11. It is worth repeating that the low level of awareness by the voters in our national survey might well reflect the fact that such pledges were not in effect in their districts – as well as the fact that they were not aware of pledges in other districts. IGE press releases on candidates signing their pledges were carried on many media outlets in the affected congressional districts but received relatively little national attention.

CHAPTER THREE: IMPACT ON CAMPAIGN CONDUCT

1. David Magleby, Kelly Patterson, and James Thurber, "Campaign Consultants and Responsible Party Government," paper presented at the annual meeting of the American Political Science Association, Washington, DC, August 27–September 3, 2000. See also, L. Sandy Maisel and Kara Z. Buckley, *Parties and Elections in America: The Electoral Process*, fourth edition, Lanham, MD: Rowman & Littlefield, 2004, Ch. 7; and James A. Thurber and Candice J. Nelson, eds., *Campaigns and Elections American Style*, Boulder, CO: Westview Press, 2004.

2. Larry Sabato, *The Rise of Political Consultants*, New York: Basic Books, 1981.

3. Lawrence Jacobs and Robert Shapiro, *Politicians Don't Pander*, Chicago: University of Chicago Press, 2000.

4. Darrell M. West, *Air Wars: Television Advertising in Election Campaigns, 1952–2004*. Washington, DC: CQ Press, 2005.

5. Amy Keller, "Direct Mail Expected to Boom in Wake of Campaign Reform," *Roll Call*, April 29, 2002, p. 1.

6. Keller, "AU Survey Underscores Split Among Political Strategists," *Roll Call*, March 13, 2003, p. 1.

7. Larry Sabato and Glenn Simpson, *Dirty Little Secrets: The Persistence of Corruption in American Politics*, New York: Times Books, 1996, p. 265.

8. Kathleen Hall Jamieson, *Dirty Politics*, New York: Oxford University Press, 1992, pp. 17–24.

9. Jodi Wilgoren, "Ethnic Comments Rattle a Congressional Race in Chicago," *New York Times*, March 6, 2002, p. A15.

10. James Thurber, Candice Nelson, and David Dulio, "Portrait of Campaign Consultants," in James Thurber and Candice Nelson, eds., *Campaign Warriors: Political Consultants in Elections*, Washington, DC: Brookings Institution Press, 2000, pp. 27–29.

11. Steven Finkel and John Geer, "A Spot Check: Casting Doubt on the Demobilizing Effect of Attack Advertising," *American Journal of Political Science*, vol. 42 (April 1998), pp. 573–595; Paul Freedman and Ken Goldstein, "Measuring Media Exposure

and the Effects of Negative Campaign Ads," *American Journal of Political Science*, vol. 43 (October 1999), pp. 1189–1208; and West, *Air Wars*.

12. There also would be a problem of multicollinearity in the regression analysis if all the reforms were put into the model simultaneously. Districts that had debates often had issue forums, and places where there were conduct codes sometimes had pledges to avoid campaign negativity.

13. Paul Abramson, John Aldrich, and David Rohde, *Change and Continuity in the 2000 Elections*, Washington, DC: Congressional Quarterly Press, 2002.

Chapter Four: Impact on Campaign Discourse

1. L. Sandy Maisel and Kara Z. Buckley, *Parties and Elections in America: The Electoral Process*, fourth edition, Lanham, MD: Rowman & Littlefield, 2004, Figure 3.1, p. 82.

2. On the first of those questions, see Paul Farhi, "Voters Are Harder to Reach as Media Outlets Multiply," *Washington Post*, June 16, 2004, p. A1.

3. Richard F. Fenno, Jr., *Home Style*, Boston: Little, Brown, 1978.

4. During the 2004 presidential campaign the Annenberg Public Policy Center of the University of Pennsylvania has run the Annenberg Political Fact Check Project, which performs precisely this function. The project grew out of frustration that the mass media were not playing this role. The project is directed by Brooks Jackson, who for more than three decades was a muckraking journalist for the Associated Press, *The Wall Street Journal*, and CNN. See their Web site at www.factcheck.org. Accessed December, 2006.

5. L. Sandy Maisel and Walter J. Stone, "Determinants of Candidate Emergence in U.S. House Elections: An Exploratory Study," *Legislative Studies Quarterly*, vol. XXII (February 1997), pp. 79–96.

6. L. Sandy Maisel, Cherie Maestas, and Walter J. Stone, "Candidate Emergence in 2002: The Impact of Redistricting on Potential Candidates' Decisions," in Thomas E. Mann and Bruce Cain, eds., *Party Lines: Competition, Partisanship, and Congressional Redistricting*, Washington, DC: Brookings Institution Press, 2005, pp. 31–50.

7. The reasoning here is quite simple. Less competitive races are less competitive, in part at least, because the candidate likely to lose does not have or does not spend much money on the campaign. Furthermore, if one is likely to lose by a great deal, or if one is likely to win by a great deal, why threaten one's own reputation by running a negative campaign? Thus, many of these campaigns are nonsubstantive, because little campaigning is done at all, but they are also not negative, for the same reason and because there are no electoral incentives to go negative.

8. However, as noted earlier, with the proliferation of media outlets and the use of them by more and more organizations, control of the intended audience has become increasingly problematic.

9. The protocol for each medium observed was developed early in the research project. Samples of each medium were sent to each of the scholars who were coding the data. Tests were done to assure intercoder reliability. All coding during the actual data collection was done by the team of scholars, with one or two political scientists responsible for each district. Intermittent tests for reliability were conducted throughout the data gathering.

10. The remaining 1 percent were paid for by or favoring independent candidates, a reflection of how few nonmajor party candidates ran serious campaigns in the districts we examined.

11. See Michael Cornfield, Democracy on Line Project, Graduate School of Political Management, The George Washington University, "The Internet and Campaign 2004: Commentary," at http://www.pewinternet.org/pdfs/Cornfield_commentary.pdf, accessed July 2006.

12. On the actual protocols, the order of the responses was varied, so that they did not always go from "worst" to "best." We have recoded here for simplicity in viewing the data.

13. Richard F. Fenno, Jr., "If, as Ralph Nader Says, Congress Is 'the Broken Branch', How Come We Love Our Congressmen So Much?" in Norman Ornstein, ed., *Congress in Change*, New York: Praeger, 1975.

14. The George Washington University, Graduate School of Public Management, Institute for Politics, Democracy & the Internet, *Online Campaigning 2002*, Washington, DC: The George Washington University, 2002; and Anthony J. Corrado and Charles M. Firestone, eds., *Elections in Cyberspace: Toward a New Era in American Politics*, Washington, DC: The Aspen Institute, 1996.

15. Viewed more positively, the Web sites do not seem to contribute to the negative nature of campaigns. Again, the reason seems obvious. If one is directing a message at supporters, why create the image that your candidate is one of those who set negative tones in campaigns. The goal should be and is to strengthen positive images.

16. A coding protocol was established, tested, and revised for the review of news coverage in much the same way as it was for campaign advertisements. In this case, the timing of news to be reviewed was revised during the data-gathering process, but it was consistent from district to district.

CHAPTER FIVE: IMPACT ON PUBLIC RESPONSES

1. Warren E. Miller, Arthur H. Miller, and Edward J. Schneider, *American National Election Studies Data Sourcebook, 1952–1978*, Cambridge, MA: Harvard University Press, 1980.

2. James Fallows, *Breaking the News*, New York: Vintage Books, 1997; and Thomas Patterson, *Out of Order*, New York: Alfred A. Knopf, 1993.

3. Larry Sabato and Glenn Simpson, *Dirty Little Secrets: The Persistence of Corruption in American Politics*, New York: Times Books, 1996.

4. Daniel Hallin, *The "Uncensored War,"* New York: Oxford University Press, 1986; and Gladys and Kurt Lang, *The Battle for Public Opinion*, New York: Columbia University Press, 1983.

5. Richard E. Neustadt, *Presidential Power and the Modern Presidents*, New York: The Free Press, 1990; and Robert E. DiClerico, *The American President*, fourth edition, Englewood Cliffs, NJ: Prentice-Hall, 1995.

6. Robert E. DiClerico, *The American President*.

7. Robert E. DiClerico, *The American President*.

8. Paul Abramson, *Political Attitudes in America*, San Francisco: W. H. Freeman, 1983.

9. Martin P. Wattenberg, *The Decline of American Political Parties, 1952–1996*, Cambridge, MA: Harvard University Press, 1998; and John R. Zaller, *The Nature and Origins of Mass Opinion*, Cambridge, England: Cambridge University Press, 1992.

10. E. J. Dionne, Jr., *Why Americans Hate Politics*, New York: Touchstone, 1991.

11. E. J. Dionne, Jr., *Why Americans Hate Politics*.

12. Michael Isikoff, *Uncovering Clinton*, New York: Crown, 1999.

13. Michael Isikoff, *Uncovering Clinton*.

14. "Timeline," *The Washington Post*, September 13, 1998, sec. A.

15. Joseph Cappella and Kathleen Hall Jamieson, *The Spiral of Cynicism*, New York: Oxford University Press, 1997.

16. There also would be a problem of multicollinearity in the regression analysis if all the reforms were put into the model simultaneously. Districts that had debates often had issue forums. And places where there were conduct codes sometimes had pledges to avoid campaign negativity.

17. Paul Abramson, *Political Attitudes in America*.

CHAPTER SIX: IMPROVING THE SYSTEM

1. Jonathan Swift, *Travels into Several Remote Nations of the World of Lemuel Gulliver*, Mount Vernon, NY: The Peter Pauper Press, 1948, p. 29.

2. Darrell M. West, *Air Wars: Television Advertising in Election Campaigns, 1952–2004*, fourth edition, Washington, DC: Congressional Quarterly Press, 2005, pp. 69–72; p. 117.

3. Richard F. Fenno, Jr., "If, as Ralph Nader Says, Congress Is 'the Broken Branch', How Come We Love Our Congressmen So Much?" in Norman Ornstein, ed., *Congress in Change*, New York: Praeger, 1975.

4. We should note, however, that candidates do have incentives to sign codes in states like Maine, in which there is a history of all candidates signing such codes. It is unclear, however, what effect these codes have. On the one hand, campaigns in Maine are – and have been for some time – closer to the model of civility and informative discourse one would like. In fact, in one of the campaigns in Maine this cycle was viewed as highly negative by many Maine citizens, but as remarkably positive by an analyst from another state who had recently moved to Maine. State-by-state experience determines what is viewed as negative. On the other hand, one of the consultants working in one of the Maine races in our sample answered that he had heard no mention of voluntary codes of conduct in the campaign, despite the fact that his candidate and that candidate's opponent both signed such a code. Given Maine's political campaign history, then, it is difficult to determine exactly what effect codes of conduct have on the campaign process.

5. Eliot Freidson, *Professionalism Reborn: Theory, Prophecy, and Policy*, Chicago: University of Chicago Press, 1994, p. 163.

6. Magali Sarfatti Larson. *The Rise of Professionalism: A Sociological Analysis*, Berkeley, CA: University of California Press, 1977, p. x.

7. David Miller, "Agreeing to Keep It Clean," *Congressional Quarterly Weekly Report*, June 19, 2004, p. 1460.

Index

Titles in the Series (*continued from page iii*)

Murray Edelman, *The Politics of Misinformation*

Frank Esser and Barbara Pfetsch, eds., *Comparing Political Communication: Theories, Cases, and Challenges*

Hernan Galperin, *New Television, Old Politics: The Transition to Digital TV in the United States and Britain*

Myra Marx Ferree, William Anthony Gamson, Jurgen Gerhards, and Dieter Rucht, *Shaping Abortion Discourse: Democracy and the Public Sphere in Germany and the United States*

Daniel C. Hallin and Paolo Mancini, *Comparing Media Systems: Three Models of Media and Politics*

Robert B. Horowitz, *Communication and Democratic Reform in South Africa*

Philip N. Howard, *New Media Campaigns and the Managed Citizen*

Richard Gunther and Anthony Mughan, eds., *Democracy and the Media: A Comparative Perspective*

Pippa Norris, *A Virtuous Circle: Political Communications in Postindustrial Society*

Pippa Norris, *Digital Divide: Civic Engagement, Information Poverty, and the Internet Worldwide*

Adam F. Simon, *The Winning Message: Candidate Behavior, Campaign Discourse*

Gadi Wolfsfeld, *Media and the Path to Peace*